Bill Summers

FULL SUN PRESS

Magic Boots

First Edition: July 2018

ISBN: 978-0-9998979-2-8

Cover and Interior Formatting: Streetlight Graphics

FULL SUN PRESS
Basking Ridge, New Jersey

CHAPTER 1

ALL EYES ON SHANNON

SHANNON SWIFT KNEW IT WAS coming. This time, she would fight back.

When that same hand grabbed her shirt, Shannon swatted it off and dashed into the box. She eyed the cross curling in behind her, and she knew this was her chance. *Here it goes...bicycle kick.*

Shannon slowed, turned her back to goal, and leaped. Leaning back in mid-air, she swung her left leg up and lashed her right boot at the ball. The goalie never moved. She'd never seen a girl shoot with her back to the net.

Like the arc of a rainbow, Shannon's shot looped over the keeper and dipped under the bar. She crashed to the turf and bit her tongue. Scrambling up, she felt the *thump-thump* in her heart, that special jolt she got after every goal. Shannon could also feel all eyes on her. By now every girl knew – this new girl could play.

Abby Rains ran up to Shannon. "Cool shot, how'd you do that?"

"Lots of practice on my trampoline, and a little luck," Shannon replied. She turned, smack into the shoulder of Chelsea Mills, the shirt-grabber. "That shot was all luck," Chelsea sassed. "You'll never do that again."

Shannon felt Chelsea's cold eyes, boring in like icicles. *Wow, this girl looks like me, tall, red hair, too many freckles. But her eyes are different.*

A whistle sounded. "Bring it in, girls," called out Kate Wiffle, coach of the Swarm, the under-twelve travel team in Manchester, New Jersey. Sixteen girls jogged toward the sideline. Fifteen were already on the Swarm, every girl but Shannon. This tryout was all about her – her chance to make the team after moving to Manchester from Tottenham, Pennsylvania. As Shannon joined the girls on the bench, one question rang in her head: *Will I make it?*

Coach Wiffle paced, her blond ponytail poking out of her yellow ball cap, the cap's crown marked by SWARM in black letters. "Good workout, just what I expect from the league champions," Coach said. "So now we start a new season. Tell me, girls, are we gonna keep our title?"

"Yes!" the girls roared. But Shannon was silent. *I'm not on the team yet. Am I?*

"I like your spirit," Coach said with a smile. "See ya next week."

The girls grabbed their bags and walked off, but Shannon froze. *Did I make it, or not?* As Coach Wiffle gathered up balls, Shannon knelt, pretending to tie her boot. Finally, she picked up her bag and stepped away.

"Hang on, Shannon," Coach called. She walked over and looked Shannon in the eye. "Thanks for coming, I'll call ya tonight."

"Sounds good, Coach. Thanks for letting me try out."

Shannon gave Coach her cell number, and then she walked toward the parking lot. Abby Rains jogged up, her blond curls swishing around her ears. Abby barely reached Shannon's chin. "Shannon, you're crazy good. You'll make the team, for sure."

"Thanks."

Just then a voice thundered across the lot. "Abby, we're leaving!"

Abby threw back her head. "Chelsea Mills, screamin' at the moon again. Anyway, see ya."

Shannon waved but her eyes were on Chelsea, standing by her car, arms crossed, scowling at Abby. Shannon frowned. *That girl is gonna be trouble, I know it.*

Shannon's mom pulled up, and she got in. "How'd it go?" Mrs. Swift asked.

"Everyone was watching me, made me nervous."

"Think you'll make it?" her mom asked as she drove out.

"Not sure, these girls are good, way better than Tottenham. Coach is calling me tonight."

"I thought you looked good," her mom said.

Shannon eyed her. "Coach has a rule, no parents at tryouts. I saw you leave."

"I watched from the woods," her mom replied. "Your bicycle kick was a gem. The two moms with me said the same thing."

"Mom, you really hung out in the woods?"

"Yep, and I have only one gripe about your play. You didn't shoot enough."

"I can't hog the ball at my tryout, Mom."

Mrs. Swift swept a shock of red hair off her forehead. “That tall girl you were playing against, she’s pretty good.”

“That’s Chelsea, the captain. She was in my face the whole time.”

“What was that about?” her mom asked.

Shannon nibbled her lip. “Maybe she’s worried because I play center-midfield. Her position.”

“That’s wild. You’re both tall, you both have red hair, and you both play center-mid.”

“Yeah, and she cheats, kept grabbin’ my shirt.”

“There’s one scoundrel on every team, Shan.”

“I wish it was only one,” Shannon shot back. “Some girl named Tory kept telling me how to play. And this Montana girl tried to trip me a few times.”

“Trip you? Come on, Shan.”

“I’ve played a lot of soccer, Mom. I know when I’m being tripped.”

Shannon squeezed her water bottle. “By the way, what’s with the name, ‘Montana?’ I mean, what’s her brother’s name, ‘Colorado’”?

Mrs. Swift snickered. “Good one, Shan.”

Shannon leaned her head on the window. "I wish we didn't move."

"But your Dad got a great job."

"But I loved Tottenham. I miss my friends."

"You'll make friends on this team."

"Maybe, but I gotta go to sixth grade in a new school."

"It's the first year of middle school, Shan. It'll be a new school for everyone."

"But I'll be the only new girl."

Shannon stuck in her ear buds for the rest of the ride. Minutes later she was standing in the shower, replaying every move she made. *I played okay, but maybe Mom's right. What if I had scored more?* Shannon shut off the shower. Toweling off, she thought she heard her phone ring. She dashed to her desk and picked it up, but there was no call. She tossed the phone into her pillow. *I'm so nervous, I'm hearing things.*

Shannon opened her shirt drawer and rummaged through until she found her only yellow T-shirt. She slipped it on. *The Swarm wear yellow shirts, maybe this'll bring me good luck.* She got dressed, flicked up a tennis ball, and started to juggle. She kept the ball up for nine touches before it hit the white carpet. Her eyes swung to her digital clock. 5:36. Shannon flopped on her bed. *Seems like time is standing still.*

"Tacos on the table!" her mom called out. Shannon grabbed her phone and bounced down the stairs. She joined Tim, her thirteen-year-old brother, and her parents at the kitchen table. Her eyes went right to her dad's new haircut.

"Dad, your hair, it's gone."

Mr. Swift smiled. "I call this my salt and pepper buzz cut. Hides the gray pretty good, huh?"

"Tim looks just like you," Shannon observed.

"Not quite," Tim shot back. "I got only pepper, no salt."

Mr. Swift chuckled at that. "So, Shan, how was your tryout?"

"I was nervous, but I think I did okay."

"You made the team, right?" Tim asked.

"I'll find out tonight, soon, I hope." Shannon spooned a line of guacamole on her taco. She was on her third bite when her phone dinged. She grabbed it, sprang out of her chair, and slipped into the family room.

Shannon could barely get out one word. "Hello."

“Shannon, it’s Coach Wiffle. I’m thrilled to welcome you to the Swarm!”

“Wow, I’m so excited!” Shannon blurted.

“So am I, Shannon. I’ll send an email to the team.”

“Thanks, Coach.”

Shannon gave Coach her email address. She clicked off, pumped her fist, and walked back to the kitchen. She tried to put on a pout, but it quickly gave way to a smile. “I made it!”

“Hooray, Shan!” Mrs. Swift roared. Shannon hugged her parents. Tim held up a palm, and Shannon rapped it. “Pretty cool, Shan, we both made the travel teams.”

Later that night, Shannon was dribbling a tennis ball across her bedroom carpet when her phone dinged. It was an email from zombie33, an address she didn’t recognize. The subject was ‘Swarm Soccer,’ so she opened it. “*No one on the Swarm wants you. Go find another team.*”

“Mom, come here!”

Mrs. Swift climbed the stairs two at a time. Shannon gave her the phone. “Read that.” Mrs.

Swift read the message, shook her head. "Who on earth would do such a thing?"

Shannon sighed. "Bet it's Chelsea Mills."

Mrs. Swift put an arm around Shannon. "I'm calling Coach Wiffle."

"No, Mom, I'll look like a sissy."

Shannon sank onto her bed. "The Swarm's been together for five years. I feel like an outsider. There must be another team I can join."

Mrs. Swift sat. "Shan, you're a great player, set all the records in Tottenham. You should play for the best team here."

"But some girls don't want me. You should see Chelsea's eyes. It's like they drill right through me."

"Come on, Shan, you'll win the girls over."

Shannon nibbled her lip. "I know you want me to play for the best team, Mom. But maybe it's okay if I don't."

Mrs. Swift rubbed Shannon's shoulder. "You've had a long day, Shan, time for bed."

Mrs. Swift walked out. Shannon rolled over, her eyes landing on the photo on her windowsill. It showed Shannon on her first soccer team, her arm around her first coach, her mom. Mrs.

Swift had played soccer in college. Her senior year, she was the top scorer in Division I. She was drafted by a pro team. But then she tore the Achilles tendon in her left leg, for the fourth and final time.

Shannon knew that her mom wanted her to be good at soccer. But no matter how well Shannon did, she felt her mom expected a little more. *Why did my mom have to be a superstar? Why do I have to live up to that?*

A bit later, Shannon dropped onto her comforter. Wiped out from her long day, she fell asleep in her T-shirt and shorts. Her light was still on.

Six blocks away, four Swarm teammates had gathered in the treehouse in Chelsea's backyard. Chelsea, Tory and Montana were trying to cheer up Cat Woods. "My mom watched the tryout," Cat said. "She says Shannon is so good, she'll take my position." Cat scooped a yellow leaf off the floor, crumpled it. "My mom knows the coach of the Monsoon. They need a midfielder. I'm trying out next week."

"No way, Cat," Chelsea shot back. "We're not letting some new girl knock you off the Swarm."

"Chelsea's right, Cat," Tory snapped. She shined her flashlight on the words Chelsea had carved on the treehouse wall: *'Chelsea, Tory, Montana and Cat – Fab Four forever!'*

"I don't know," Montana muttered. "Shannon is good, I mean, really good."

"She's not that good," Chelsea argued.

"You ever see a bicycle kick like that?" Montana countered.

Chelsea smirked. "That was a fluke. Besides, she's a ball hog."

"She passed to me, a lot," Montana fired back.

Chelsea paced. "Look, I already sent her a message telling her not to join. Made up an email address – she'll never know who sent it. Bet that scares her off."

"What if it doesn't?" Cat asked.

"We go to our back-up plan," Chelsea replied. "We tell Coach that Shannon's not a good fit, that she breaks up our midfield."

"Won't work," Montana whined.

"Okay, Mon," Tory blurted, "you got any bright ideas?"

"I got one," Chelsea cut in, a sly grin edging across her face. "I'll take her down."

Montana's eyes bulged. "You mean, hurt her?"

"I'll do a slide tackle – get her ankle."

"Good idea, Chelse," Tory agreed.

But Cat frowned. "It's not gonna work. I'm gonna be playing against you guys."

"No way," Chelsea railed. She stuck a finger at her friends. "We got our plan, girls. One way or another, Shannon Swift is goin' down."

CHAPTER 2

HALEY AND HER PUMPKINS

SHANNON WOKE THE NEXT MORNING, the email nagging her like a thorn. She buried her face in her pillow. *This is crazy, why is someone trying to scare me off?*

Shannon sat up, peeled back her window shade, and gazed at her new backyard. Everything from her old yard was missing. There was no "Square," the mini-soccer field littered with cleat marks. There was no trampoline, the springs worn thin from Shannon's bicycle kicks. There were no friends.

But Shannon saw one thing she didn't have in Tottenham. A sea of weeds. She slumped on her bed. *I had the coolest yard in Tottenham. Here, I got a thousand dandelions crowding out a few blades of grass.*

Shannon heard pans rattling in the kitchen. She got up and went downstairs, found her dad opening a carton of eggs. "Hey, Shan, scramble you an egg?"

"Okay," Shannon said, her voice flat.

"Shan, you okay?" her dad asked.

"I don't like it here, Dad. I mean, that email is creepy."

"I bet it was just a prank," her dad said. "Some girl is mad because you're better than she is."

Shannon sat, her gaze swinging to the backyard. "I miss our old yard, Dad. I mean, look outside. The dandelions are having a party, and everyone came."

Mr. Swift chuckled. "We'll get those weeds out, Shan. Look, this yard is perfect for another Square. The goals are coming tonight, the trampoline tomorrow."

Her dad put the egg in front of Shannon. She looked at it. *Scrambled, just like my brain.* Shannon thought about her tryout. She had spent only two hours with Chelsea Mills. But she felt like she'd always known her – and never liked her. Then there was Tory the know-it-all, and Montana, the tripper. *It's like they rounded up all the bullies in Manchester and put them on the Swarm.*

Shannon's mom stepped in. "Shan, I went for a walk this morning and met our neighbor next door, Sarah Punt. Her daughter, Haley, plays keeper on the Swarm. They invited us to stop over later."

"Sounds good."

"Did you meet Haley at your tryout?"

"Yeah, but I didn't talk to her."

Shannon stuck in a forkful of egg. *Hope Haley's okay. Some girls on this team have to be okay, right?*

That afternoon, Shannon and her mom walked next door and rang the doorbell. A tall woman with short black hair answered, her white apron smudged with cookie dough. With a big smile, she blared, "Welcome to the neighborhood!" Mrs. Punt eyed Shannon. "Haley said you were awesome at the tryout." Shannon beamed. *I like Haley already.* Mrs. Punt went on. "She's in her room, why don't you run up?"

Shannon climbed the stairs. At the top she found Haley hanging from a pull-up bar, her legs bent, her face red as a tomato. "What are you doing?" Shannon asked.

"Three more seconds," Haley whispered. She closed her eyes and held on a bit longer. Finally, she dropped and blew out a long breath. "I hang from there every day for thirty seconds," Haley said, flipping her dark brown pigtails over her shoulders. "Makes my arms longer. The longer my arms, the more balls I can reach."

Shannon grinned. "So Haley, you always been a goalie?"

"Yeah, with a name like Punt, my parents figured it was my natural position."

"Good one!"

Haley waved Shannon into her room and they dropped into facing bean bag chairs. Shannon eyed the scrapbook on Haley's table, a team photo of the Swarm on the cover, under the words, SWARM, LEAGUE CHAMPIONS.

"That's our scrapbook from last year," Haley said. She handed it to Shannon. "Take a look." Shannon leafed through newspaper clippings, until she got tired of seeing pictures of Chelsea. "The Swarm is an amazing team," Shannon said.

"Yeah, and with you, we're gonna be

unstoppable," Haley followed. "That bicycle kick you scored on me, I never saw it coming. You froze me like a statue."

Shannon snickered at that. She pointed at the photo on the scrapbook cover. "Tell me about the girls, Haley."

Haley put a finger on Abby Rains. "Small but scrappy, and a crack-up." Haley moved her finger to Olga Watts. "Good defender, but bossy." Haley pointed at Montana Brown. "Great dribbler, friends with Tory and Chelsea, but not as nasty." Tory Smoot was next. "Scoring machine, but ice cold, and best friends with Chelsea." Finally, Haley pointed at Chelsea. "Chelsea Mills, best player in the league, but angry and mean."

"Chelsea sassed me at the tryout," Shannon said.

"I bet she sees you as a threat."

Shannon bit her lip. *Should I tell Haley about the email? I hardly know her, better not.* Shannon eyed a photo on the wall, showing Haley sitting on a huge pumpkin. "Cool pumpkin," Shannon said.

"Biggest one ever out of our patch, twenty-six pounds."

"You grow pumpkins?"

"Yeah, in the field past our backyard." Haley stood. "Come on, let's check 'em out."

Shannon sprang up and followed Haley downstairs and through a door off the kitchen. At the back of the yard they crossed a footbridge spanning a shallow creek. Across the bridge sat a field with a bunch of small hills, crisscrossed by vines with little green leaves. Haley swept her hand across the field. "That's our pumpkin patch. We plant six seeds on each hill. In a good year, we grow about sixty pumpkins."

"That's so cool," Shannon exclaimed. "What do you do with 'em?"

"We sell 'em at my dad's place, Punts' General Store. Mom lets me keep the money."

"Wow, your dad has his own store?"

"Sure does, I'll take you there."

Shannon noticed a cluster of bees swarming around the leaves. "How do you keep the bees away?"

"We need those bees, Shannon. Pumpkin plants have boy flowers and girl flowers. The bees gather pollen from the boys and give it to the girls. It's called pollination, and it's happening right now. That's how the pumpkins start to grow."

Shannon nodded. *Pollination, big word, too big to remember.* Past the field she saw a small red barn, surrounded by a fence with white posts. Near the fence, a white cow with black spots grazed on tall grass. "That your cow?" Shannon asked.

"Yep, we got four of 'em. My dad makes ice cream in that barn, sells it at his store. Wanna try some?"

Shannon's jaw fell open. "You know it!"

Haley broke into a trot across the bridge, Shannon clinging to her heels. When they reached the kitchen, Haley opened the freezer and got out three cartons – Bear Paws, Chocolate Drizzle, and Peanut Butter Burst. Shannon dug out a scoop of Bear Paws – vanilla with chunks of fudge. She popped in a spoonful. "Yum, so creamy."

"Straight from the cows," Haley said. "Best ice cream in town, maybe the country."

Shannon reloaded her spoon. "Haley, you should come over tomorrow. My dad's gonna build the Square."

Haley scrunched her face. "The Square?"

"It's a mini soccer field. We had one in our old backyard."

"Sounds cool," Haley replied as she spooned out the last dollop of Peanut Butter Burst. Shannon finished her ice cream, and soon after she headed for home. Walking up the stone path to her porch, she looked back at the Punts' house. *Made my first friend, Haley Punt.* Up the porch she hopped, two steps at a time.

The next morning, Shannon woke to the rumble of a truck pulling up the driveway. She peeled back the curtain. *The trampoline is being delivered!* Her mom and Tim were on their knees in the yard, using prongs to coax out the weeds. *I gotta help.* Shannon pulled on a ratty pair of jeans and an old sweatshirt. When she reached the yard, Tim tossed the prong to her. "I dug up a hundred and thirty weeds. But don't worry, there's another five hundred for you."

Shannon noticed the goals sitting at the back of the yard. *We're gonna make a new Square!* She knelt and dug out her first weed. About an hour later, Shannon spooned out what she thought was the last yellow invader. But then she spied another one. *Weeds are tricky, there's always another one sprouting up somewhere.*

By mid-afternoon, the entire Square was free of weeds. That's when Mr. Swift wheeled his lawn tractor out of the shed. Shannon ran up to him. Over the roar of the engine, she yelled, "Cut it nice and short, Dad, like your hair." He stuck up a thumb. After Mr. Swift finished mowing the grass, he rolled out one hundred and twenty yards of yellow chalk. Next, he set up a large goal on the back line. On the other sides, Shannon and Tim placed smaller goals. The Square had come to life.

Later that afternoon, Shannon and Tim played keep-away from their mom. Mrs. Swift chased hard, but she couldn't get a foot on the ball. Finally, she threw up her hands. "I give up, you kids are too quick."

Mr. Swift stepped onto the deck with a pitcher of lemonade. "Come and get it!" he yelled. Shannon raced over. Her dad handed her a glass, and she guzzled it in one tilt. "Thanks for your help today, Shan."

"This is awesome, Dad, just like our old yard."

After dinner, Shannon went upstairs to

check the notes on her wall calendar. Three 'firsts' jumped out at her.

First practice – Wednesday, September 3

First game – Saturday, September 6

First day of school – Wednesday, September 10

Shannon looked out at the sun, sitting low in the sky. *My first practice is tomorrow, I need to get a few more touches before dark.* Shannon called Haley, and ten minutes later they met in the backyard. When Haley saw the Square, her mouth fell open. "Hey, this Square thing is cool!"

Shannon had scattered ten balls twenty yards from the big goal. Haley settled in between the posts, and Shannon blasted away. She stuck her first three shots in the corners. The next two she thumped over the bar, and then Haley blocked the next two. Shannon drilled the next shot right at Haley's face. She got her hands up just in time, but the force of the ball knocked her to the ground. Haley put up her arms. "I surrender."

Shannon trotted over and helped Haley up. Haley held out her palms. "See how red my hands are? That never happens. You smash the ball harder than anyone."

Shannon didn't answer. She was chewing her lip, staring into the grass. "Shannon, you okay?" Haley asked.

"I'm nervous about practice tomorrow," Shannon admitted.

"Why?" Haley asked.

"I got an email. It said the Swarm doesn't want me."

Haley crinkled her nose. "That's insane, who sent it?"

"Nobody signed it."

"Maybe it's Chelsea Mills." Haley guessed. "She has a wicked temper, like a volcano. Some girl kept tripping her in a game last year. Chelsea kicked her so hard, almost broke her leg."

Shannon's eyes flared. Haley put up her hands. "Don't worry, Coach Wiffle's the boss. She puts up with nothin'."

"Glad to hear that, Haley."

Haley rested a hand on Shannon's shoulder. "My friends call me Hale. So call me Hale, okay?"

"Sure, Hale, and you call me, 'Shan.'"

"You got it, Shan." They collected the balls,

and then Haley headed for home. Shannon went in, found her mom in the kitchen. "I was watching you and Haley," Mrs. Swift said. "You kicked a few balls over the top. I think you were leaning back."

Mom's spying on me again. "I'm not some robot, Mom."

"Just trying to help, Shan."

Mrs. Swift eyed the clock on the wall. "Shan, your first practice is tomorrow. You better get to bed soon. I know how important tomorrow is to you."

Shannon rolled her eyes. *Important to me, or to you?* She went up, brushed her teeth, and changed into her pajamas. Shannon climbed into bed and turned off her light. Even in the dark, she could see Chelsea's face. *That girl is scary. She doesn't like me, at all. And we're teammates?*

Shannon rolled over. *There are thousands of towns in New Jersey. Why does Chelsea Mills have to live in Manchester? What did I do to deserve that?*

CHAPTER 3

CLOSE ENEMIES

SHANNON KNEW IT WAS A bad habit – chewing her lip when she was nervous. But when she got to Freedom Park for her first practice with the Swarm, her lip was getting a workout. *Back home, I never had to prove myself. But now I'm the new girl, and I don't like being new.*

Coach Wiffle called the team in. "Girls, let's welcome the newest member of the Swarm, Shannon Swift." As Coach led the cheers, Shannon noticed that Chelsea was the first to stop clapping.

Coach peeled off her jacket. "Okay girls, time to stretch."

"Come on, Coach, we're already loose," Abby whined.

"No, you're not," Coach shot back. "Think about a piece of bubble gum. When you put gum in, you can't blow a bubble right away, can you? You have to soften it up first. Think of your body the same way. You've got to loosen up your muscles before you use them."

Shannon nodded. *Comparing your body to a piece of gum, I gotta remember that one.*

After the girls finished stretching, Coach pulled red and yellow T-shirts from her bag. Shannon put on red, along with Chelsea, Tory, Montana, Cat, and three other girls.

Coach spoke. "On red, Shannon will play in the middle. Chelsea's on the right, Tory's on the left."

"But, Coach, I'm always in the middle," Chelsea whined.

"Let's mix it up," Coach answered.

Shannon looked at Chelsea, and felt her frosty glare.

The girls lined up. Coach punted the ball high and yelled, "Game on!" Shannon cushioned the punt on her thigh, led Chelsea into the corner, and darted toward the box. Chelsea crossed, but a defender headed the ball clear. "Come on, Shannon, make your run earlier!" Chelsea yelled.

"Sorry," Shannon replied. But then she wished she hadn't. *Make the run earlier? I got there as fast as I could. Why is Chelsea bossing me like she's the coach?*

A minute later, Tory stole a pass near the sideline. Shannon ran into open space ahead of Tory. "Tory!" she called, but Tory passed back to a teammate.

"Don't yell out, Shannon," Tory said. "You alert the other team."

Shannon bit into her lip. *Don't call for the ball? These girls are nuts!*

Feeling a blast of adrenaline race through her, Shannon stole a pass and dribbled toward goal. As a defender closed in, Shannon saw Cat running free on her right. She led Cat into the box, but Cat slowed and the keeper beat her to the ball. "You gotta pass sooner!" Cat grumbled.

"You gotta finish your run!" Shannon shot back. Shannon hung her head. *I keep getting yelled at. Am I screwing up?*

After twenty-five minutes, neither team had scored. "Five more minutes, girls," Coach called out. "I wanna see a goal!"

A minute later, Shannon gathered a loose ball and swept it into open space down the flank. “Now!” Tory yelled as she sprang toward the corner. *No, Tory, I’ve had enough of your games.* Shannon dribbled around a defender and cut in toward the box. Seeing the keeper far off her line, she stubbed her boot under the ball. It rose over the keeper’s hands and ducked inches under the bar, a perfect “rainbow” from sixteen yards.

Abby ran over. “Great shot!” But Tory met Shannon with a sneer. “I was open, you shoulda passed.”

“I had a good shot,” Shannon fired back.

“So it’s all about you, huh?” Tory dished back.

Abby glared at Tory. “She scored, Tory. What’s wrong with you?”

Coach Wiffle blew her whistle and called the girls in. “Get a drink and sit on the bench.”

Shannon jogged off, grabbed her water bottle, and squeezed out the last few drops. *This is crazy. I never got yelled at back home, why am I getting yelled at here?* She saw Chelsea, Tory, Montana, and Cat, huddled at the end of the bench. Shannon figured they were talking about her. She wished she could be a fly on Chelsea's shoulder.

Chelsea whispered, "Okay, girls, time for our back-up plan. We tell Coach that Shannon's not a good fit."

"Let's do it," Tory agreed.

"Coach won't go for that," Montana countered.

Chelsea glared at Montana. "Mon, we owe this to Cat. We've been friends since kindergarten, right?"

"But what if Shannon turns out to be okay?"

Chelsea jabbed Montana's shoulder. "It's not about Shannon, it's about Cat. As soon as practice ends, you follow me, got it?" The girls nodded.

Coach scanned her clipboard. "Girls, we're one of eight teams in the Morris Hills league. We play each team once this fall. The top two teams qualify for a regional tournament in Washington, D.C. Tell me, are we going to Washington?"

"Yes!" the girls hollered.

Coach smiled, and then her eyes rested on Shannon. "Shannon, I teach English at Manchester High School. I love words, and I use words to help us focus. Today's word is 'SELFLESS.' It means caring about others, and not worrying about yourself. Anyone know why I chose that word?"

Abby's hand shot up. "Because we have to support each other, especially our new teammate."

"That's right, Abby." Coach ran her eyes across Chelsea, Cat, Montana, and Tory. "I heard a lot of nonsense today. Girls giving a teammate a hard time, for no good reason. That ends today, got it?"

The girls nodded, and Coach swung her eyes back to Shannon. "Shannon, you played great today. We're lucky to have you on the Swarm."

Shannon smiled inside. *Coach Wiffle is awesome.*

Coach checked her watch. "That's it for today, see you tomorrow."

As Shannon picked up her bag, she noticed that Chelsea, Tory, Cat, and Montana had surrounded Coach. She wished she could listen in, but she was too far away. Still, her ears were burning.

"Coach, that new girl has no clue," Chelsea wailed. "She kept getting in my space."

"Yeah, she plays too slow," Tory piled on.

Cat was next. "She plays rough – fouled me like, five times."

Montana told the final fib. "I was open a lot, but she didn't pass."

Coach Wiffle curled her lips until they disappeared. "Girls, that is a bunch of poppycock. Shannon is scary good. She'll give us a fresh spark, make us much better."

"But Coach, we won the league without her," Chelsea sniped.

"That's enough, Chelsea."

"But –"

"No more 'buts,' girl!" Coach grumbled. "The only butt to worry about is yours. Keep acting like this, and your butt goes on the bench."

Chelsea stalked off, with Tory, Cat, and Montana trailing her. In the parking lot, Haley caught up to Shannon. "Shan, you were the best player, even better than Chelsea."

"Thanks, Hale." A bit later Mrs. Swift pulled up, and Shannon got in. "How'd it go?" her mom asked.

"Weird," Shannon replied. "Some girls yelled at me. Said I was out of position, said I didn't pass."

"That's not you, Shan."

"Chelsea's a good player, Mom, but she doesn't like me, I can feel it."

"Bet she's jealous," Mrs. Swift shot in.

"Maybe, but I don't like getting yelled at by my teammates."

"You score any goals?"

Shannon flipped her head back. "Why is it always about scoring?"

"Well, you score a lot, Shan."

"I scored one, that good enough?"

"That's fine, Shan," her mom answered. Then she changed the subject. "School starts next week. We need to buy your supplies."

"With my luck, those four brats will be in all my classes."

"Be positive, Shan. School will give you a chance to meet new people."

"Whatever," Shannon groused, and then she stuck in her ear buds.

That night, Chelsea, Tory, Montana and Cat met in Chelsea's tree house. "We're running out of time," Cat said. "I'm trying out for the Monsoon in two days."

Chelsea cracked a smile. "Don't worry, Cat, cuz tomorrow, I'm takin' Shannon down."

“What if you really hurt her?” Montana asked.

“I won’t, just gonna scare her off.”

“But remember that girl on the Cheetahs?” Montana followed. “You almost broke her leg.”

Chelsea waved that off. “That girl was after me, I had to get her first.”

“I think it’s a bad idea,” Montana went on. “Coach will be watchin’, you know.”

“You think I’m scared of Coach Wiffle?” Chelsea popped off. “She’s like a wiffle ball, soft and full of holes.”

Chelsea leaned into Montana’s face. “Look, girl, we made a deal. And tomorrow, I’m getting rid of Shannon Swift.”

The next morning, dark clouds hung low as the girls gathered for practice. Coach Wiffle chose up teams. Shannon and Chelsea would face each other at center midfield. Shannon bit into her lip. *Chelsea tackles hard, I gotta be alert.*

A sprinkle wet the grass as the girls took the field. Shannon tapped the opening kick to Abby and swung out wide. Abby spooned a high ball down the flank. Shannon chased it, Chelsea fast on her heels. Shannon reached the ball first. As she tapped it ahead, Chelsea slid in and rammed her ankle. “Aaah!” Shannon yelled as she dropped in a heap.

Coach Wiffle blew her whistle. She ran over and knelt by Shannon. “How bad is it?” she asked.

Shannon swung her ankle in a circle. “Better sit for a while.”

Shannon got up and limped off. Coach fetched her a bag of ice from a cooler, and Shannon pressed it on her ankle. Then Coach blew her whistle and called Chelsea over. Chelsea jogged up, and Coach glared. “That was a reckless tackle,” Coach snapped. “Never again.”

“But you tell me to go in hard.”

“Go hard for the ball, not the leg,” Coach shot back. “I’ve got my eye on you, girl.”

Chelsea said nothing. Shannon had heard it all. *At least Coach has my back.*

When Chelsea scored minutes later, Shannon stood and put weight on her leg. It hurt a bit, but not enough. She jogged over to Coach Wiffle. “Coach, I’m good to go.”

“No, you’re done today.”

"But I want to play. I *need* to play."

Coach stared into Shannon's eyes. "You sure you're okay?"

Shannon answered with her feet, dashing onto the field. A few minutes later, she swiped the ball from Cat and dribbled free down the flank. Glancing over her shoulder, Shannon saw Chelsea closing fast. When Shannon pulled her leg back, Chelsea slid. This time, Shannon was ready. *The frog.* She squeezed the ball between her boots and jumped, the ball still between her feet in mid-air. Chelsea slid under Shannon, her cleats flashing high. Shannon came down and cut in toward the corner of the box. She looked up, chose her window, and lashed her right instep into the ball.

Boom! It was a clean strike, flush off the shoestrings. The ball knuckled past the keeper and thumped the net in the far corner. Coach blew her whistle. "Great shot, Shannon. Play on, girls. Chelsea Mills, get over here!"

Chelsea jogged to the sideline. Coach met her with an icy stare. "You're done for the day, Chelsea."

"But I went for the ball!" Chelsea protested.

"No way," Coach fired back. "Your cleats

were up, just like when you cut Shannon down before. You ever go after a teammate again, I'll kick you off the team."

Coach dug through Chelsea's bag, pulled out her phone. "Call your mom, now. When we play our first game on Saturday, you better show me that you still want to be on this team."

Chelsea made the call, picked up her backpack, and stormed off. Shannon looked over just as Chelsea tossed up her water bottle and punted it. It flew end over end and clanked on a see-saw.

The girls scrimmaged for another half-hour before Coach called them in. "Our first game is Saturday against the Rampage, so it's time for a penalty kick contest. We take turns. You miss once, you're out. Last girl standing takes our PKs in games."

"But Chelsea took our PKs last year," Tory snapped. "She's not even here."

"That's her problem, not yours," Coach fired back.

After seven rounds, only two girls had made all their shots. Shannon and Tory. As Shannon stepped up to the ball, Tory whispered, "You'll blow this one." Shannon smiled. *Go ahead,*

Tory, fire me up. Shannon cracked a low shot to Haley's right. Haley guessed right, her body sliding toward the shot. But the ball squirted under her armpit and hit the net. Shannon was relieved – and surprised. *I thought Haley had that.*

Now the pressure was on Tory. She fired hard to Haley's left, but Haley was moving that way. She tipped the ball into the post and it bounced back onto the field. Tory dropped to her knees, and Coach blew her whistle. "Great save, Haley. Shannon, you'll take our penalty kicks. Now bring it in."

Coach paced, her eyes on the grass. "Girls, I'm too steamed to think of a word right now. We're done, good night."

Shannon walked off, and Haley jogged up. "I've never seen Coach Wiffle so angry."

Shannon nodded. "And I've never seen a player sent home from practice."

Haley put a hand on Shannon's shoulder. "I'm glad you won the contest."

"I couldn't believe my last shot got past you, Hale."

"It's like Coach says, Shan. Sometimes, you gotta put your teammate first."

Haley winked, and Shannon smiled back.

That night at dinner, Tim shared exciting news. He had scored the winning goal in his team's first game. "My wing set me up on the doorstep, easy tap-in. The guys pass and move really well."

Shannon looked at her brother. "So Tim, you think I could join your team?"

Mr. Swift chuckled. "How did your practice go, Shan?"

"Chelsea tried to wreck my ankle, twice."

Tim pounded the table. "That girl's crazy, you never go after a teammate."

"Look at it this way, Shan," Mrs. Swift chimed in. "Chelsea will make you stronger."

"Come on, Mom, that girl's scary."

"You want me to call Coach Wiffle?" her dad asked.

"Coach knows what's going on," Shannon said. "She kicked Chelsea out of practice. Later, I won the penalty kick competition. Chelsea took 'em last year."

"You should be taking them, Shan," her mom said. "You never miss."

Shannon pushed a few peas around her plate. *I wonder how Chelsea will react when I take the penalty kicks?*

She would soon find out.

CHAPTER 4

TROUBLE FROM TWELVE YARDS

On Saturday morning, Shannon opened her eyes to a sliver of sunlight cutting across her purple comforter. She rolled up her shade and gazed up at a big blue sky. *Perfect day for my first game.* She hustled down to the kitchen and found her dad fixing her usual pre-game breakfast – two blueberry pancakes, a sliced banana, and a piece of wheat toast topped with peanut butter.

"Morning, Shan, fired up to play?" he asked.

"Sort of."

"Sort of?" her dad echoed.

Shannon sat. "I got butterflies in my belly, Dad. What if my teammates yell at me?"

Mr. Swift poured grapefruit juice into Shannon's favorite glass – the one with an etching of U.S. national team star, Alex Morgan. He put the glass and a full plate in front of Shannon and sat opposite her. "Shan, if a teammate makes trouble, I'm sure Coach Wiffle will be on top of it," he said.

"Hope so." Shannon drizzled cinnamon syrup on her pancakes, cut through the stack four times, made sixteen pieces. Mr. Swift laced his fingers on the table. "I know soccer hasn't been easy, Shan. I'm proud of how you've handled things."

"Thanks, Dad. You always listen, and you never put pressure on me. I like that."

After she ate, Shannon climbed the stairs and put on her uniform. Yellow socks, yellow shorts, and a yellow shirt, all in black trim. She slipped on a yellow headband and looked in the mirror on the back of her door. *The Swarm, now I get it! We're a swarm of yellow jackets. And today, we're gonna sting the Rampage.*

Shannon took her soccer boots from her bag and pulled out the soiled white laces. She got out a pair of the yellow laces her mom gave her and held them against her shirt. *Mom's amazing, the colors are a perfect match.* She ran the laces through her boots and stuck them in her bag.

When the Swifts pulled into Freedom Park an hour later, Shannon could feel the butterflies flapping away. "Have a great game, Shan," her mom said, "and put a few in the net."

Shannon got out and slammed the door. *I got the butterflies, and Mom makes 'em flap even faster.* She jogged to the bench, and she and Abby fell into an easy lap around the field. A bit later Coach Wiffle called the girls in. "I have some news," Coach said. "Cat Woods has left the team. She joined the Monsoon."

Chatter ran through the huddle. Shannon felt prickly stares from Chelsea and Tory. *This is crazy. I have enemies – on my own team.* Coach raised her hand to hush the talk. "Let's focus on the game. I want you to attack from the start. Remember, our confidence is their doubt."

Coach stuck out a hand, knuckles up, and each girl added a hand to the stack. "One, two, three, SWARM!" As Shannon took the field, she glanced to the sidelines. Her dad was in his usual spot, camera in hand. He nodded, and she nodded back. *Okay, Shannon, just play your game.* In the second minute, Shannon collected a loose ball in the circle. She fed Tory and darted up the right flank. As Tory dribbled toward the box, Shannon broke free on her right. Tory tried to split two defenders, but the ball got jarred away. Shannon ran up. "Look for me, I was open."

Tory scowled. "You didn't say anything. I didn't know you were there."

Shannon jogged off, her lips curled shut. *The last time I called for the ball, you told me not to say anything.*

Two minutes later Shannon picked off a pass, blew past an opponent, and set up Montana ten yards from goal. Montana had an easy finish, but she spooned the ball over the bar. A minute later, Shannon slithered past two foes and fed Montana at the penalty spot. But Montana leaned back and fired high again. "Dang!" Montana wailed, jerking her head away.

Shannon ran over. "I got something for ya at halftime, Montana."

Soon the ref's whistle signaled the end of a scoreless half. Shannon hustled to the sideline and dug through her bag. She pulled out her spare pair of yellow laces and stepped over to

Montana. "I used to shoot high a lot," Shannon said. "Then I put in a pair of bright laces, like these. When you shoot, keep your eyes on your laces. Your head stays down, and the ball stays low."

"Thanks," Montana said, and she quickly changed her laces.

Early in the second half, Abby settled a bouncing ball on her thigh and bolted down the flank. Shannon burst into an open seam and Abby floated the ball ahead of her. Shannon gathered on the run and tore past a defender. Crossing into the box, she looked up, picked her corner, and unleashed.

Thwack! Shannon struck the ball so hard that no one moved, not even the keeper. Shannon watched her shot fly straight at the far post. *Go in, ball!* The ball rattled the wood and ricocheted into the net. Swarm 1, Rampage 0.

Shannon got mobbed by most of her teammates, even Montana. But as she emerged from the huddle, she noticed that Chelsea and Tory had jogged back to their positions. *Those girls are so cold. But at least Montana is warming up.*

Ten minutes later the Rampage earned a corner kick. As their wing stepped toward the ball, the girls being marked by Shannon and Chelsea ran to change places. "Shannon, switch!" Chelsea yelled.

Shannon picked up the girl running to the near post, but Chelsea stayed with her too. The ball sailed to the unmarked player at the back post, and she nodded in the tying goal.

Tory ran over to Shannon. "Shannon, that was your player! Come on!"

"Chelsea said to switch!" Shannon shot back.

Tory had already turned away. Abby ran up to Shannon. "I heard Chelsea say 'switch.' I can't believe she did that."

A minute later, Shannon made a jarring tackle and looked up to see Montana running toward the box. Shannon chipped over the center back, the ball landing in Montana's path. Montana tapped it once and cocked her leg, telling herself, *Don't look up until you see yellow.*

Boom! Montana cracked a low bolt that sizzled past the keeper into the far corner. Swarm 2, Rampage 1.

Montana ran over and leaped on Shannon. “I saw yellow on that one!”

Shannon looked toward the sideline, where her dad held up three fingers. Three minutes left in this see-saw game. Would the see-saw be still now, or would it tilt again?

The Rampage battled hard for the tying goal. Their left wing crossed into the box, but Olga smashed it all the way to the circle. Shannon pumped her fist. *That should do it.* The Rampage center back ran up and swept her boot into the bouncing ball. The ball sailed high and far, knuckling toward the net. Haley scrambled back and leaped, but the ball squeezed between her fingers and the bar. Swarm 2, Rampage 2. Shannon threw her head back. *That shot was a fluke!*

As Shannon jogged back to the circle, Chelsea ran up. “Get me the ball, I’ll win this thing.”

“Okay, Chelsea, you’re on.”

Abby tapped to Shannon. She wriggled around an opponent and spotted Chelsea, racing down the flank like a yellow blur. Shannon lofted a high ball toward the corner. Chelsea ran onto it and flashed past a defender into the box. She pushed the ball past another girl, but the girl stuck out her boot and clipped Chelsea to the grass. The ref blew his whistle – penalty kick for the Swarm.

Chelsea got up. She grabbed the ball and placed it on the penalty spot twelve yards from goal.

"Shannon, your kick!" Coach Wiffle called out.

Chelsea stared toward the bench, her mouth agape. "Say what? I take the PKs."

"Not anymore," Abby said. "We had a contest at practice, Shannon won."

"But I wasn't there!" Chelsea blared.

Shannon stepped toward the ball, but Chelsea blocked her. "I got taken down. I'm takin' the kick."

Shannon felt her heart pound. "Coach says it's my kick."

Chelsea glared. "Coach is wrong."

Abby stepped up. "Chelsea, you heard Coach, it's Shannon's kick."

Chelsea stuck out a finger. "Back off, girls."

The ref blew his whistle. "Get on with it!"

Shannon and Abby backed away. Chelsea lined up behind the ball. She stepped up and smashed a hard shot. The keeper didn't bother to move. The ball flew five feet over the bar. A minute later, the game ended. Swarm 2, Rampage 2.

Shannon walked off, and Olga ran up. "You shoulda taken that kick."

"I tried," Shannon replied.

"Not hard enough," Olga snapped. "You can't let Chelsea walk all over you."

Shannon closed her eyes. *Haley's right, Olga is bossy. This team has a lot of bosses.*

As the girls reached the bench, Coach met Chelsea with a hard stare. "Did you hear me say that was Shannon's kick?"

"I took the penalty kicks last year, made 'em all," Chelsea sassed.

Coach stepped closer, her nose an inch from Chelsea's. "Who's the coach of this team?"

Chelsea stared back. "You are, I'm afraid. I mean, we beat this team by three goals last year. Then you make all these changes, and look what happens. Crazy."

Coach opened her mouth, but swallowed her words. She turned to face the team. "Girls, my word for today is, 'IRATE.' It means really, really ticked, and that's what I am right now."

Coach tugged her cap over her eyes. “That’s it for today. Except for you, Chelsea, you stay here.”

Shannon and the other girls picked up their bags and began to walk away. Coach waited for a bit, and then she leaned into Chelsea’s face. “You crossed me, Chelsea Mills. You do it again, and I’ll kick you off the team.”

Chelsea locked eyes with Coach. “You can’t, I quit.”

When Shannon reached her family, her anger spilled out. “That was my penalty kick!”

“Did Chelsea ever blow it,” Tim cracked. “That shot almost cleared the moon.”

“That girl has some nerve,” Mrs. Swift added. “What did Coach say after the game?”

“Chelsea did most of the talking, said Coach was crazy.”

“She’s nuts!” Tim wailed. “No player talks to a coach like that.”

Shannon took the last gulp from her bottle. “You know the corner kick they scored on? Chelsea told me to switch, but she didn’t. Her player scored, and she tried to blame me.”

As they got in the car, Mr. Swift tried for a positive spin. “Shan, your goal was a gem.”

“Yeah, but after I scored, Chelsea and Tory didn’t come near me.”

“Face it, Shan,” Tim shot in, “you’re better than they are, and they can’t stand it.”

“But we’re on the same team!” Shannon could feel her face heating up. Her mom was about to send her into full boil.

“I can’t remember the last time you scored only one goal,” Mrs. Swift needled.

“You better get used to it, Mom,” Shannon fired back. “This isn’t Tottenham anymore.”

Mr. Swift jumped back in. “Shan, you got your head on a lot of crosses.”

“Yeah, but I headed three balls over the bar.”

“I’ll help you with your headers,” Tim offered. “Let’s hit the Square when we get home.”

“I’m too pooped, maybe tomorrow.” Shannon closed her eyes. *Chelsea is crazy, just crazy. I can’t play with her. What am I gonna do?*

Later that afternoon, Shannon got a text from Haley. Pumpkin duty. Eager to get her mind off the game, Shannon jogged over and met Haley in her backyard. “Hey, Shan, sorry about the game.”

Shannon tilted her head. “Sorry about what, Hale?”

“I strayed too far off my line on that last goal.”

Shannon waved a hand. “Come on, Hale, that was a wicked shot, got caught up in the wind. You needed stilts for that one.”

Haley chuckled. As they neared the bridge, Shannon swung her foot through the grass. “Besides, I didn’t play so great. My mom can’t remember the last time I scored only one goal.”

Haley picked up a rock and tossed it in the creek. “Your mom is whacko, Shan. I mean, your passing was magic. Montana coulda scored six goals off your feeds. And I know you woulda made that PK. Could you believe Chelsea? My dad says she’s bad for the team.”

“Yeah, I wonder what Coach said to her.”

When they reached the patch, Shannon’s eyes lit up. “The pumpkins are getting bigger!”

Haley bent over one. “Some pumpkins are leaning, like this one. We need to move ‘em so they sit square. That way they grow round, not lopsided. Watch.”

Haley lifted the stem and turned the pumpkin. The bottom sat square, the stem pointing straight up. Shannon thought of one of her dad's sayings: *Aim for the sky.* The girls took turns until they had all the stems pointing straight up. Haley ran a sleeve across her brow. "I think we've earned a treat, Shan. My dad brought home a new flavor he's testing, Peanut Brittle."

"Peanut brittle, what's that?" Shannon asked.

"It's vanilla with strips of peanuts and caramel. It's called brittle because the strips break easily. Wanna try some?"

Shannon answered with her feet. She sprinted toward the Punts' house, Haley a few steps behind.

A few blocks away, Chelsea, Tory, and Montana had gathered in the treehouse. "I got some news, girls," Chelsea announced. "I have a new team – the Monsoon."

Montana's jaw dropped. "No way."

Chelsea nodded. "Cat told me her coach kicked three girls off the team cuz they wouldn't quit lacrosse. My mom called their coach. He has a uniform for me."

"Does Coach Wiffle know?" Montana asked.

"She knows I'm not on the Swarm. I quit after the game today." A sly grin edged across Chelsea's face. "Guess who the Monsoon plays in three weeks?"

"The Swarm?" Montana guessed.

"You got it," Chelsea replied. "October seventh, Freedom Park. I can't wait to line up with Cat, Tory, and Montana, against our old team."

Montana's eyebrows shot up. "What do ya mean?"

"The Monsoon has two more openings," Chelsea went on. "You and Tory are coming with me. We said we'd stick together, no matter what."

"I'm in," Tory vowed.

Chelsea fixed her gaze on Montana. "Well, Mon?"

Montana blew out a long breath. "I'm not sure what to say."

Chelsea gripped Montana's shoulders. "It's easy, Mon. Just say, 'Yes.'"

Montana thought about the yellow laces Shannon gave her. She thought about all her friends on the Swarm. She thought about what a bully Chelsea had become. "I'm staying with the Swarm," she said.

Chelsea shook her head. "Wrong answer, Mon. You got ten seconds to change your mind."

But Montana didn't need ten seconds. "I'm staying, that's it."

Chelsea pushed Montana away. "Get out of my treehouse, and never come back."

CHAPTER 5

SHANNON FEELS THE HEAT

THAT SUNDAY, SHANNON WAS PICKING out notebooks at the store when it hit her: *I no longer dread going to school on Wednesday. Soccer's been everything since I moved, and not such a good thing. I'm ready for something else.*

Shannon turned a corner and came upon a huge wall of hi-liters. She scanned her options – yellow, green, pink, blue, orange, purple. She called Tim over. "Help me pick a color."

Tim ran his eyes across the wall. "It was easy when they only made yellow, now you got the whole rainbow. How about yellow or orange?"

Shannon flipped a coin. It came up heads, and she tossed a sleeve of yellow hi-liters into the cart. Tim eyed the packet.

"Figures," he said. "Your hi-liters, your uniform, your shoelaces, even the chalk on the Square. You're the queen of yellow."

Shannon laughed. "Guess I gotta paint my bedroom yellow."

Tim waved a hand. "You're bananas."

"Hah, good one!"

The Swifts snaked through every aisle, stuffing the cart with notebooks, pens, hi-liters, and wall calendars. As they stood in line, Mrs. Swift bounced a palm off her forehead. "Forgot one thing," she said, scooting off. A minute later she trotted up with a small notebook.

"Who's that for?" Shannon asked.

"It's for me, so I can keep notes when you and Tim play."

Shannon rolled her eyes. "Mom, aren't we a little old for that?"

"Only trying to help, Shan."

Shannon looked at Tim. He shrugged, and then pointed at the notebook. "At least the paper's not yellow."

When the Swifts got home, Shannon told Tim she was ready for that heading lesson. They went out to the Square, where Tim fished a ball out of the net. "You kept heading the bottom half of the ball," Tim said. "That's why it went over the bar."

"So what should I do, head the middle?" Shannon asked.

"Yep, the ball will shoot straight off your head. Let's try some."

Tim dribbled to the corner and floated a cross in front of the goal. Shannon ran on and snapped her forehead into it. The ball nicked the bottom of the bar and settled in the net. Tim served three more crosses. Shannon nodded each one on a line into the twine. Tim jogged over. "I think you got it."

"Wow, what a difference," Shannon said. "Thanks for the tip."

"Any time, Shan. That'll be ten bucks."

"Hah, very funny."

Shannon dribbled a ball toward the trampoline. "I'm gonna hit some bicycle kicks, wanna join me?"

Tim waved. "I've tried that kick, it's crazy hard."

"Come on, I can help."

Tim turned for the garage. "Nah, I'm goin' for a real bike ride."

Shannon climbed on the trampoline, bounced

the ball on the soft rubber floor, and watched it rise overhead. When the ball reached its apex, Shannon jumped and leaned back. She swung her left leg up and snapped her right foot into the ball.

Wham! The ball jabbed the net circling the trampoline. Shannon did seven more – four stingers and three flubs. After the last one, she flicked up the ball and climbed off, a smile on her face. *The more I practice, the better I get.*

When Shannon got to practice on Monday, she noticed that Chelsea and Tory weren't there. *That's weird, they're always the first ones here.* Minutes later, Coach Wiffle asked the girls to sit on the bench. Coach paced, her arms crossed. "I have some news. Chelsea and Tory have quit the team."

Shannon's jaw dropped. But then she felt a bolt go through her – a bolt of joy. Coach went on. "Chelsea and Tory are good players, but they weren't good teammates. Chelsea never accepted losing her position to Shannon. And that stunt she pulled with the penalty kick, I've never seen anything like it. As for Tory, I'm afraid she lets Chelsea intimidate her. Whatever Chelsea does, Tory seems to follow."

"We're better off without 'em," Haley snapped.

"Did they go to another team?" Olga asked.

"They joined the Monsoon," Montana cut in.

Coach turned to Montana. "The Monsoon, that's Cat's new team, right?"

"Right," Montana answered. "We play 'em in a few weeks."

Shannon felt her pulse race. *I wonder what's worse, playing with Chelsea, or playing against her?*

Abby eyed Montana. "Montana, you're like, best friends with Chelsea, Tory, and Cat. How come you didn't go with 'em?"

Montana gazed into the grass. "They wanted me to, but I decided to stay."

Montana looked at Shannon. "Besides, Chelsea was wrong. And I was wrong."

Coach walked up and put an arm around Montana. "Mon, we're glad you stayed. I'm proud of you for standing up to Chelsea Mills."

"But Coach, now our lineup has a big hole in the middle," Olga pointed out.

"Brooke and Tess will join Shannon and Montana in midfield," Coach said.

"But then we have no one coming off the bench," Olga whined.

"I've called a few girls from tryouts. We'll add a few players."

Olga, again. "Chelsea and Tory scored like a billion goals. Who's gonna score now?"

"Abby and Montana have proven they can score," Coach answered. "Plus, I know Shannon will score a ton."

Shannon felt her heart thump. *Score a ton?*

Abby stood. "I know one thing. When we play the Monsoon in two weeks, Chelsea, Tory, and Cat are goin' down."

The girls hooted, and Coach peeled off her jacket. "I could use a little exercise. Come on, let's run a few laps."

As the team fell in behind Coach, Montana jogged up to Shannon. "I'm sorry, Shannon."

"Sorry for what?" Shannon asked.

"You know, I was kinda nasty to you."

Shannon flipped a hand through the air. "Don't worry about it, Mon. I could tell you didn't really mean it. I'm glad you're still here."

"Thanks, I know I made the right decision."

Later, Coach set up a scrimmage, and Shannon felt like she had been set free. *No more teammates yelling at me, or chopping me down.* She ran hard, but never felt winded. She scored two goals, and set up two more. After she smashed in her last goal, Coach blew her whistle and called the girls in.

"Shannon, come here," Coach called out. Shannon felt her face go flush as she stepped to Coach's side. Coach put a hand on her shoulder. "Shannon had a boot in four goals today. You know why?"

"Because she's really good," Abby cracked. The girls laughed, and Coach put up her hand. "Yes, Shannon is really good. But she's also assertive. Anyone know what that means?"

The girls exchanged puzzled looks, and Coach went on. "ASSERTIVE. It means, 'confidently aggressive.'" Coach let her words sink in. "When Shannon sees a teammate get the ball, she doesn't watch, she moves. She asserts herself."

Shannon felt her ears tingle. But Coach wasn't done. "Girls, Shannon *wants* the ball. Great players don't wait for the ball to come to them. They thrust themselves into the game."

Coach ended practice a minute later. As Shannon gathered her bag, she felt a thorn poking her side. She kept thinking about Coach's words. *Chelsea never accepted losing her position. Whatever Chelsea does, Tory seems to follow.*

Shannon frowned. *I took Chelsea's position. Chelsea and Tory left the team because of me. So did Cat.*

That wasn't the only thorn. *Coach said I'll score a ton of goals. Gosh, it's hard enough dealing with my mom.*

While the other girls headed for their rides, Shannon hovered near the bench. Coach Wiffle was stuffing the last ball into her bag when she noticed her. "Shan, what's up?"

"I hope you're not mad at me, Coach."

Coach tilted her head sideways. "Why would I be mad at you?"

"I kinda screwed things up. If I didn't move here, Cat, Chelsea and Tory would still be on the team."

Coach motioned toward the bench, and they sat. "Look, if Chelsea hadn't quit, I was gonna kick her off the team," Coach said. "Truth is, I'd rather have you than Chelsea, Tory, and Cat.

I mean, you're the best dang eleven-year-old I've ever seen. And the great thing is, you don't even know how good you are."

Shannon felt her heart hammer. "I'm not *that* good. You say I'll score a ton of goals. What if I don't?"

"Just do your best, Shannon. I know we'll like the results. Deal?"

"Sounds good, Coach."

Shannon started to stand, but Coach put a hand on her shoulder. "One more thing. I have a special guest coming to practice Wednesday. I know you'll like what he has to say."

Shannon's eyebrows shot up. "Who is it?"

"Oh no, I can't ruin the surprise."

Shannon hustled over and hopped in the car. "Dad, get this, Chelsea quit the team, so did Tory."

"Wow, Shan. How do you feel?"

"I felt weird at first, but Coach said it wasn't my fault."

"Coach is right," Mr. Swift said. "Those girls were selfish. They put themselves ahead of the team."

"Coach also said it's okay if I don't score a

lot," Shannon added. "But I think she expects me to."

Mr. Swift looked at her. "Remember how we dealt with that in Tottenham?"

Shannon thought about the talk she had with her dad a year ago.

Dad, every time I score, people expect more.

Shan, you always try your best. That's all that matters.

But people think that if I don't score, I had a bad game.

Ignore them, they don't know soccer. The world's best strikers don't score in half their games.

Shannon smiled. *It's great to have a dad who gets it.*

After dinner that night, Shannon went up to her room and got out her notebook. She wrote down Coach's word. *Assertive – confidently aggressive.* She looked at the other words on her list. *Selfless. Irate. Coach knows a lot of cool words. How does she remember 'em all?*

Minutes later Shannon's phone dinged, an email from Chelsea. *Nice going, Swift. You move to Manchester and break up the best team in the league. Guess who the best team is now? That's right, the Monsoon. I can't wait to play against you. We're gonna crush the Swarm, and I'm gonna crush you!*

Shannon pitched her phone into her pillow. *That girl really bugs me. When I see her in school on Wednesday, I'm gonna stand up to her, right?*

CHAPTER 6

BAD LUCK IN GEOGRAPHY CLASS

On Wednesday, Shannon stirred twenty minutes before her alarm was set to go off. She reached up and shut it off. *Hah, who needs an alarm on the first day of school?* She eyed the clothes sitting on her chair, faded blue jeans, a sky-blue long-sleeve shirt, and dark blue high-top sneakers. She swung out and got dressed. Scooting downstairs, she told herself not to think about Chelsea. *That's dumb, I'm thinking about her. What if she's in one of my classes? What if she's in all of them?*

Shannon ate only a few spoonfuls of her cereal and three slices of her banana. A knot rising in her throat, she hugged her parents at the door. Stepping into a drizzle, Shannon pulled up the hood on her jacket. Up ahead she spied Haley waiting on the sidewalk, and she trotted up. The girls matched strides to the corner, shared a seat on the bus, and jabbered all the way to school. Inside, they came to a four-way intersection. Shannon went one way toward her homeroom, Haley went the opposite way toward hers. Shannon looked over her shoulder and saw Haley disappearing into the crowd. She bit her lip. *I wish I could stay with Haley all day.*

Shannon weaved around kids clustered in the hallway. She didn't recognize anyone, and no one said a word to her. *This is creepy. Back in Tottenham, the first day of school was like a party. Here, I'm surrounded by strangers. It's like I'm invisible.* But when Shannon walked into English class ten minutes later, she was the center of attention.

"You Shannon Swift?" asked the boy seated next to her.

"Yeah, how'd you know?"

The boy swept thick blond bangs off his forehead. "My sister plays on an under-eleven team. All the girls are talkin' about you. Guess you're pretty good."

Shannon smiled. "Nice to hear."

"I'm Tommy," the boy went on. "I play striker for the Manchester Meteors."

"And I'm Andy," said the boy on her other side. "I'm the goalie. We were undefeated last year."

Shannon noticed Andy's black hair, running to his shoulders. *His hair is longer than Haley's.* "You must be really good," Shannon said.

"Yeah, wicked good," Andy agreed.

An awkward silence hung in the air. Shannon eyed the clock. *I swear that second hand is ticking through syrup.*

The bell finally rang. Shannon glanced quickly at each boy. *Wow, these boys already know me. Kinda cool, but kinda weird.*

After third period, Shannon counted up her good luck. Four classes, no Chelsea, no Tory, and no Cat. She headed for the cafeteria, where she met Haley under the American flag hanging in the corner. They got lunch and joined four other Swarm teammates at a table. As Shannon sipped her milk she spotted Chelsea, Tory, and Cat across the room. *The farther away, the better.*

After lunch, Shannon's luck held. Seven classes – no brats. *Seven down, one to go.*

Shannon hustled to geography class and sat in the front row. She glanced around. *No Chelsea, this is awesome.*

The bell rang, and Mrs. Hooper rose from behind her desk. Her gray hair pulled up in a bun, she wore a red blouse tucked into a long plaid skirt. She walked back and closed the door. When she got back to her desk, the door swung open. Shannon looked back, and in walked Chelsea Mills.

Chelsea sat in the back row, right next to Abby. Abby frowned at Shannon, and Shannon fought off a grin. A bit later, Mrs. Hooper turned to write on the blackboard. That's when Shannon felt a wad of paper hit the back of her head. Giggles grew into laughs.

Mrs. Hooper faced the class. "What's so funny?" she asked. Abby started to raise her hand, but Chelsea kicked her calf. Mrs. Hooper looked for a clue on the faces in front of her, but saw none. Shannon sat still as a goalpost. *My face feels like it's on fire.*

Mrs. Hooper walked to the middle of the room. "Get your laughs out now, kids, because I won't put up with any more nonsense."

When class ended, Mrs. Hooper asked

Shannon to stay. While her classmates walked out, Shannon stirred in her seat. *Oh boy, I hope she doesn't think I started trouble.* Mrs. Hooper sat. "Shannon, you were the only one who wasn't laughing. Do you know what happened?"

"I think someone threw a piece of paper. It hit my head, good shot."

Mrs. Hooper nodded. "Sometimes new students get picked on. Don't worry, I'll put a quick end to it."

"Thanks, Missus Hooper."

Mrs. Hooper smiled. "You'll like it here, Shannon. Let me know if I can help with anything, okay?"

"Sounds good." Shannon walked out. *I made it to my last period, and then my luck ran out.* On the bus ride home, Shannon thought ahead to soccer practice. *Wonder who the special guest will be?* At home she changed into her gear, and her mom drove her to Freedom Park. Shannon and Abby were heading a ball back and forth when Coach Wiffle called the girls in. "We have a guest coming at the end of practice. But first, let's scrimmage."

A few minutes into the game, Coach whistled play to a halt. "Come on girls, I feel like I'm watching a dribbling contest," she complained. "I mean, four of you have already lost it on the dribble."

Coach rolled a ball to Shannon and backed off thirty yards to the sideline. "Shannon, when I say 'go,' dribble as fast as you can to this sideline." Coach clicked her watch and yelled, "Go."

Shannon took off, pushing the ball with the outsides of her feet until she crossed the line. Coach checked her watch. "That took five-point-seven seconds. Now dribble back to where you started."

Shannon tapped the ball thirty yards off. "Okay," Coach said, "pass to me, hard and low." Shannon thumped the ball to Coach. She controlled it and checked her watch. "One point six seconds."

Coach flicked the ball up and caught it. "Girls, one-point-six is way better than five-point-seven. Remember, think pass first, dribble second. That's how you play this game."

The girls scrimmaged for another thirty minutes before Coach set up a shooting drill. Haley got in goal, and the girls lined up thirty yards away. Coach stood on the penalty spot, a few balls at her feet. "I'll feed each of you a ball just over the eighteen, and you strike it first-time. Let's start with the left foot."

Abby groaned. "Come on, Coach, you know we got no left feet."

The girls roared. Coach started the drill. The first two shots drifted wide, the next two ballooned over the bar. When Olga made it five flubs in a row, Coach blew her whistle. "Girls, you haven't tested Haley once. She could be sitting in a lawn chair, painting her nails. Look, I know you don't like to use your left foot. But you need to work on your weak foot, until you don't have a weak foot."

Olga put up a hand. "My dad says some of the best players use only one foot."

"True, Olga, but most top players are good with both feet," Coach said. "Look at our national team. Carli Lloyd, Megan Rapinoe, Tobin Heath, they're all two-footed. Trust me, two good feet are better than one."

Coach paced. "Aha, I just thought of my word for the day, 'AMBIDEXTROUS.' It means skilled with both hands – and both feet."

Abby smirked. "Big word, Coach, too big for my brain."

The girls snickered. Just then a black sports car swung into the lot. The girls watched as a man got out and jogged toward the field. He wore soccer gear, even cleats. Coach greeted him with a hug. “Girls, meet Jack Dash. He coaches the Wave, the top under-thirteen academy team in New Jersey. He kindly offered to share a few tips.”

Coach Jack shook hands with each girl and then asked them to sit. “Girls, the best players use all their weapons. Let’s start with the foot. Who can name each part of the foot used in soccer?”

“The inside, the outside, and the instep,” Abby said.

“Good start, five more.”

Abby made a sour face. “Eight parts? You got a different foot.”

The girls laughed, and Shannon raised her hand. “The heel, the bottom, and the toes.”

Coach nodded. “Very good. Two to go.”

No one spoke. Coach tossed a ball in the air. As it neared the ground, he raised his leg and ‘caught’ the ball on top of his foot.

“The top!” Olga blurted.

“Got it! Now, the last part. Watch this.”

Coach Jack dribbled toward the girls and pulled his leg back as if he was about to blast the ball right at them. The girls covered their faces, but he slowed his leg. Rather than kick the ball, he used the outer edge of his big toe to tap the ball behind his planted leg. It was a perfect fake-out.

"Cool move!" Abby blared.

Coach Jack lifted his boot and tapped the outside of the bone below his big toe. "You can learn to use this bone to trick your opponent – take the ball in a direction she doesn't expect."

Abby raised a hand. "Coach, you said the toes are one of the eight parts. But you don't kick the ball with your toes."

"But you do *poke* with them, Abby. Sometimes, that's the only way to reach the ball before your opponent does."

Coach eyed the girls. "What's the most important space on the field?"

"The penalty boxes?" Olga guessed.

"Good try."

"The midfield?" Shannon offered.

"Another good guess, but the space I'm thinking about is about six inches wide." The field went quiet, until Coach tapped his ears. "Between your ears!" Haley blared.

"Right on, Haley," Coach Jack said. "Your attitude is everything. You're league champs – I'm sure your opponents try to bring you down. Trash talk, maybe a stray elbow, knee or boot. Always stand up for yourself. Never feel bad about being good."

Shannon nodded. *It's like he knows about Chelsea and me.*

Coach paced. "Have you ever been told that you should've played better, when you *know* you tried your best?" A bunch of hands went up, and Coach went on. "When I was your age, I scored three goals in a game. Some kid said I should've scored six, and he was my teammate! Don't let people hang unfair expectations on you. Do your best, and shut out the rest."

This is wild, Shannon thought. *It's like he knows about my mom.* Shannon glanced over at Abby. She was yanking up blades of grass. "Coach, I feel like I'm in a classroom," Abby whined.

"Abby!" shouted Coach Wiffle.

"Sorry!"

"Last thing," Coach Jack said. "Soccer's

a funny game. Sometimes, the better team doesn't win. One time my team controlled the whole game, hit the post about ten times. The other team scored on a fluky shot from midfield. That's soccer. If it happens, accept it and win the next game."

Shannon thought about the game versus the Rampage. *We owned them, and they tied us on that wind-blown shot.* Coach Jack picked up his bag. "I'm off to scout a player," he said. "Her name's Chelsea Mills. I hear she's the best scorer in the league, and I need a scorer on my state team."

Shannon's eyes bulged. *Chelsea Mills?* The girls cheered as Coach Jack jogged off, but Shannon felt like she had taken a punch to the gut. *He's scouting Chelsea? Why isn't he scouting me?*

Coach Wiffle spoke. "Girls, like Coach Jack said, believe in yourself. When you do that, you can do anything, on or off the field. That's it for today."

A bit later Mr. Swift pulled up, and Shannon got in. "Dad, the coach of the state's top under-thirteen academy team was here. He had this great line, 'Do your best, and shut out the rest.' But get this, he's going to scout Chelsea Mills."

"Really?"

"Yeah, he says he needs a scorer for his team. Guess he doesn't know about me. But wait 'til he sees what I do on Saturday."

CHAPTER 7

GIRLS VERSUS BOYS

COME SATURDAY MORNING, SHANNON COULDN'T wait to get to Freedom Park. The sun was out, and the butterflies in her belly had stopped flapping. *No more Chelsea, no more Tory. I can relax and have fun.*

Shannon played with no fear, and no doubt. Ten minutes in, she lashed a dart from twenty yards that knuckled over the keeper's hands and stung the net. Five minutes later, Shannon stole a back-pass and broke in alone. When the goalie charged off her line, Shannon calmly chipped the ball over her and under the bar.

Early in the second half, Shannon leaped over a defender and nodded Abby's corner kick into the corner. In the last minute Shannon swiped a pass in the circle, barreled ahead, and uncorked a rocket from thirty yards. The ball rang the post and Abby tucked in the rebound. Swarm 4, Fury 0.

After the final whistle, Coach Wiffle called the team in. "Fabulous game, girls. My word for the day is, 'RESILIENT.' It means you bounced back in the face of a challenge. We lost two players this week, but you believed in yourselves. I love your attitude, love your hustle. See you Tuesday."

As Shannon reached the lot, she was met by three big smiles. "Shan, you were awesome!" Mr. Swift raved.

"Thanks, Dad, I felt free out there."

Mrs. Swift hung an arm around Shannon's shoulders. "You banged in three goals. That's the Shannon Swift we're used to."

"Yeah, too bad Coach Jack wasn't here to see it."

"That was some header you scored," Tim said. "Guess I'm a pretty good coach."

"Ha, ha," Shannon cracked, "you're still not getting ten dollars."

"Ten?" Tim grumbled. "That lesson was so good, I deserve twenty."

"You're not getting a dime, bro. I'll show you how to do a bicycle kick, then we're even."

The next morning, Shannon went downstairs to find Tim reading the local paper, *The Manchester Mirror*. Tim handed it to Shannon. "You're famous, Shan. Now you owe me thirty dollars."

Shannon looked at the page. A large color photo showed her leaping high to head in her third goal.

"Wow, that picture is crazy huge," she said.

"That's nothing," Tim replied. "Read the story."

Shannon started with the headline.

SWARM MAKE 'SWIFT' WORK OF THE FURY

She read the story. *Newcomer Shannon Swift scored three goals and set up another, pacing the Swarm to a 4-0 win over the Fury yesterday. Swift's goals came in every flavor. She buried a bomb from twenty-five yards, chipped a rainbow over the keeper, and nodded in a corner kick. Swift joined the Swarm this summer after moving from Tottenham, Pennsylvania.*

"Shannon is a special player," said Coach Kate Wiffle. "When she gets the ball, you can see the energy rise in her teammates."

Left wing Abby Rains set up Swift's last goal. "Shannon has magic boots," Rains said. "She does stuff we've never seen before."

Shannon beamed. *Magic boots! Chelsea's gonna love this.*

Shannon studied the league standings under the article. With one win and one tie, the Swarm sat tied for third place. A bit later, Shannon was peeling a banana when Haley called. "Shan, you see the paper? Great picture, you must be three feet off the ground. And I loved Abby's quote."

"Thanks, Hale, the quote's kind of embarrassing."

"Come on, Shan, you are like magic. Hey, I'm gonna work some magic on the pumpkins. Wanna come over?"

"On my way!" Shannon gobbled her banana, downed a glass of grapefruit juice, and darted out. She met Haley in her backyard and followed her into the Punts' shed. Haley grabbed two pairs of gloves and tossed one pair to Shannon.

Next, she took hand clippers off the wall and set them in a wheelbarrow.

"It's clean-up day," Haley explained as she steered the wheelbarrow out. "The vines grow like crazy. We have to prune the little vines that grow off the big vines."

"Why's that?" Shannon asked.

"Cuz the vines get all tangled and the pumpkins don't grow right."

When they reached the patch, Haley pointed to a spot where vines darted off in all directions. She got down on a knee and snipped off a cluster of small vines. Shannon followed Haley to another spot, and this time Shannon knelt and clipped a few vines. On her last snip, a nettle poked through a hole in her glove. "Whoa, these vines have sharp edges."

Haley nodded. "Yeah, kinda like Chelsea's elbows."

When the girls finished pruning, the wheelbarrow overflowed with vines. Haley pushed it past the patch and dumped it out. She slapped her gloves, knocking bits of dirt loose. "Now comes the sad part, Shan. We need to remove the bad pumpkins, the ones that are turning yellow and shriveling up."

"Why's that?" Shannon asked.

"Cuz the bad ones take away nutrients from the good ones."

Shannon nodded. *It's like the Swarm. Gotta get rid of the selfish players, so everyone else can grow.* Shannon watched as Haley cut loose a few small, wrinkly pumpkins. Taking turns, the girls removed thirteen pumpkins, enough to fill the wheelbarrow to the brim. Haley steered it out back and dumped the spoiled pumpkins next to the cut vines. She pointed at the pile. "I call those 'lumpkins.' Not quite good enough to be pumpkins."

"Hale, you come up with some crazy words."

Haley clapped her gloves again. "Shan, the best part comes next week. We'll each pick a pumpkin and carve our names in 'em."

"Cool!"

Minutes later Shannon started for home, her hands and arms caked with dirt. She walked in the kitchen and held out her arms for her dad to see. "Digging around the pumpkin patch, eh?" Mr. Swift asked.

"It's a blast, Dad. Haley really knows her stuff, and I'm learning a lot."

Mrs. Swift walked in, holding the *Manchester*

Mirror. "Shan, I just read the story on your game," she said. "I guess when you score three goals, you get the headlines."

"Guess so, Mom. But I bet I get teased tomorrow."

Shannon was right. On Monday in English class, the boys circled around. "Saw your name all over the paper," said Tommy Hayes, the left wing for the Manchester Meteors.

"You must be pretty good," added Andy Mack, the goalie.

"We have a good team," Shannon replied.

Andy nodded. "Maybe so, but you know our team would crush you."

Shannon tilted her head. "Crush us, really?"

"Yeah, like an elephant stepping on a grape," Andy sniped.

Now Shannon's fuse was lit. "I bet our keeper and I could beat you two in a penalty-kick contest."

"Hah!" Andy volleyed. "Tommy, you hear that?"

"I think I heard it, but I must be dreaming," Tommy cracked.

"You're not dreaming, Tommy," Shannon fired back. "You're having a nightmare."

"Ooh, pretty cocky, huh?" Tommy said.

"Confident, not cocky," Shannon replied.

"Your keeper's Haley Punt, right?" Tommy asked.

"That's right."

Tommy flashed a crooked smile. "You want me to shoot from thirty yards away?"

"Doubt you could reach the goal," Shannon snapped back.

Andy cut in. "Okay, Shannon, you're on. Friday, after school, on the field behind the gym."

"It's a deal," Shannon agreed.

"Wait a minute," Tommy added. "You lose, and you and Haley gotta be ball girls at our next game."

Shannon thought fast. She knew that Haley's dad printed T-shirts at his store. "We win, and you have to wear T-shirts we make. I mean, put 'em on, right there on the field."

"Fine," Andy agreed. "But don't waste your money on shirts that'll never be worn."

News of the contest shot through school. It was the talk of the table at lunch, and two of Shannon's teachers asked her about it. On the bus ride home, a boy asked Shannon if she expected to win. Her answer: "With Haley between the posts, I always expect to win."

That afternoon, Shannon and Haley met on the Square. First, they brainstormed what message to put on the T-shirts. Then Haley called her dad's shop and placed the order. She hung up and pumped a fist. "They're gonna make the shirts tonight."

"Great," Shannon said. "Let's practice our PKs."

Haley crouched between the posts, and Shannon fired away. She scored on her first three shots, but then she eased up a bit, and Haley saved two of the next three. *Good, I want Haley to be confident against the boys.*

All week Shannon's mind was stuck on the contest. With everyone asking her about it, she could think of little else. When the final bell rang on Friday, she hurried out of geography class. But when she reached the hall, she stepped into an ambush. "You and your penalty-kick contest," Chelsea sassed. "What a showboat."

“You don’t have to go,” Shannon fired back.

“Oh, yes I do,” Chelsea retorted. “Can’t wait to see you and Haley get creamed.”

Chelsea leaned into Shannon’s face. Shannon tried to hold her stare, but she blinked.

“So, Swift, your name’s all over the paper. Think you’re a big star, huh? I’m gonna –”

Chelsea stopped when a large hand landed on her shoulder. It was Mr. Armstrong, Shannon’s gym teacher. “Can I help you with something, Chelsea?” he asked. Chelsea stormed off.

“Thanks, Mister Armstrong,” Shannon said.

“No sweat, Shannon,” he replied. “Hey, I hope you and Haley win today. Those boys have swelled heads. They can barely fit through the locker room door.”

Shannon snickered. Hustling down the hall, she looked out at the crowd gathering on the hill between the gym and the field. Shannon reached the locker room, where Haley was doing her stretches on the floor. “I’m nervous, Hale,” Shannon admitted as she changed. “The whole school’s out there. I even saw Principal Potts.”

“Relax, Shan. The T-shirts are in my bag. In twenty minutes, the boys get to put them on.”

Shannon laced her boots tight. On her right

boot she tied the knot on the outside, away from her instep. The girls walked out, and a mix of cheers and jeers rose up. Shannon followed Haley through the crowd. *There are more people here than at our games.* The girls met Tommy and Andy on the penalty spot. Tommy laid out the rules. "Five shots for each team. We take turns. The team with the most goals wins."

Tommy flipped a coin and Shannon called 'heads.' It landed on tails. "You shoot first," Tommy said.

As Andy took his spot on the line, the crowd fell silent. Andy clapped his gloves, the noise echoing off the gym's huge brick wall. Shannon lined up behind the ball. She took a deep breath. *Why am I so crazy nervous?* She stepped up and shot low to her left. Andy dove and smothered the ball.

A chant rose out of the crowd. "Andy, Andy, Andy!" Shannon felt her face turn red. *Okay, that's the only one I'll miss.*

Tommy set his ball on the spot and backed away. As he stepped toward it, he saw Haley leaning to her left. Tommy drilled hard and low into the other corner. Boys 1, Girls 0. Shannon and Tommy both made their next two shots.

Going into round four, the boys led, 3-2. As Shannon approached the spot, she swept a trickle of sweat off her forehead. *Gotta make this one.* She put her ball down and decided, *left side high.*

Andy must have read her mind. He dove toward her shot, but it rose over his hands and punched the roof of the net. Shannon clenched her fist. As Tommy stepped up, Shannon ran over to Haley. “He’s shot to your right all three times,” she whispered. “He’ll probably do it again.”

As Tommy stepped into the ball, Haley dove right. But Tommy shot left. Too far left. The ball rattled the post and kicked onto the pitch. The crowd went wild, the cheers and boos drowning each other out.

Now it was 3-3, one round to go. Shannon set up behind the ball, her eyes locked on the left corner. But then she stepped up and shot to her right. Andy dove the wrong way and tasted dirt. But Shannon’s shot flew wider than she wanted. The ball struck the inside of the post and bounced on the goal line. Shannon froze. The ball hit the other post, landed on the line again, and finally trickled over.

"Andy!" Tommy hollered, "you shoulda dove on it!"

The girls led, 4-3. The boys were down to their last shot. "You can do it, Hale!" Shannon shouted.

Tommy put the ball on the spot. Haley crouched. As Tommy neared the ball, Haley leaned to her left. But then she dove right – right at Tommy's shot. Haley reached as far as she could. She ticked the ball with the tip of her middle finger, pushing it inches outside the post.

The girls won. Tommy fell to his knees. Shannon ran up and hugged Haley. "Fabulous save, Hale!"

"Good thing I hang from my pull-up bar, right, Shan?" Haley got her bag and took out two black shirts with large yellow lettering on the front and back. She tossed one to each boy, and they put them on. "Walk toward the crowd, boys," Haley said.

As the boys trudged toward the hill, the crowd read the front. WE GOT SWARMED ON

"Now turn around," Haley instructed.

The boys turned their backs so the crowd could read the words: GIRLS RULE! This time, the entire crowd burst into cheers. Climbing the hill, Shannon and Haley got mobbed by their friends. But the last girl to meet Shannon wasn't there to congratulate her. "You're still a loser, Swift," Chelsea snapped. "When we play you a week from Saturday, I'll prove it."

Shannon felt herself tense up. She tried to respond, but the words got trapped in her throat. As Chelsea marched off, Shannon's fear turned to anger. *Come on, Shannon, fight back!*

That night, Mr. Swift made Shannon's favorite meal – tacos and chocolate milkshakes.

"How did your shootout go against the boys?" Mrs. Swift asked.

"We won," Shannon said as she dumped a pile of guacamole on her plate.

"It was hilarious," Tim piped in. "The boys had to put on shirts that said, 'Girls rule.'"

Mr. Swift eyed Shannon. "Shan, you don't look very excited."

Dad always knows. "Beating the boys was great, but then Chelsea Mills had to ruin it. Called me a loser, said the Monsoon will crush the Swarm."

Shannon fired her napkin on the table. "Today it was girls against boys, and who was Chelsea rooting for? The boys."

"Remember Jack Dash's words," her dad said. "Sometimes, when others aren't as good as you, they try to take you down."

"Back home, the girls weren't as good as me," said Shannon. "They never acted like this."

"You're new here, and you've changed things," her dad replied. "Some people don't like change, not when they get knocked off the hill."

Shannon took a long drink of her shake. "Sometimes, I wish I wasn't so good."

Tim thumped a fist on the table. "That's how Chelsea wants you to think. You can't let her drag you down. You gotta fight fire with fire."

"It's not that easy, Tim," Shannon griped.

"Come on, Shan, think about when we go one-on-one on the Square. You always give it back to me, so give it back to her."

Mrs. Swift looked at Shannon. "Shan, when I was your age, I had some jealous teammates. I tried to change at first. I didn't play so hard. I passed when I should've shot."

"What happened?" Shannon asked.

“I felt terrible, about myself,” her mom said. “I realized I had to be me, do my best, all the time.”

“What about the jealousy?” Shannon asked.

“I decided not to be friends with jealous people,” her mom replied. “I stood up to them. After a while, they left me alone. I hung out with my real friends, people who wanted me to do well.”

Shannon nodded. She finished her shake, stood, and went up to her room. Shannon checked the Swarm’s schedule on her bulletin board. They would play the Cheetahs the next day.

Dropping on her bed, Shannon thought about the pile of ‘lumpkins’ she and Haley had tossed out. *Chelsea is trying to make me shrivel up, like one of those little yellow lumpkins. No way. I’m gonna win the scoring title. I’ll show Coach Jack that he should be scouting me, not Chelsea.*

CHAPTER 8

SHOELESS SHANNON, CLUELESS CHEETAHS

THE CHEETAHS' COACH HAD READ the *Manchester Mirror.* She knew about Shannon, and she had a plan to stop her. She called it, "The Swift Sandwich."

From the opening whistle, two Cheetahs put the squeeze on Shannon. She tried to shake them with zigzagging runs, but the girls stuck to her like spots on a Dalmatian. After five minutes Shannon had touched the ball only once. When the ball rolled out of play, she called in Abby and Montana.

"Those girls are on me like Velcro. I'll stay wide on the left side, pull 'em out. You can go two-on-one against their left back. I'll try to beat those girls into the box and meet your crosses."

Abby and Montana ruled the right flank

and sprayed balls into the goalmouth. But the Cheetah goalie owned the box. On every cross, she bolted off her line and snagged the ball before Shannon could get there. As the clock ticked down, Shannon felt her frustration mount. *It's almost halftime, and I haven't done a thing yet!*

In the stands, Mrs. Swift wrung her hands. "Shannon's like a ghost out there."

"Chill, Mom," Tim told her. "She's got two quick girls on her. Her teammates have to step up."

Late in the half, the Swarm earned a corner kick. As Abby lined up behind the ball, Shannon hopped on her toes. *Now's my chance.* Abby floated her kick toward the back post. From opposite sides, Shannon and the keeper went up together. *Wham!* Shannon went down like a sack of potatoes.

The keeper had punched the ball away. On her follow-through she socked Shannon in the eye, by accident. Shannon lay dazed. Coach Wiffle ran out.

"Shan, can you hear me?" Coach asked.

Shannon's eyes flicked open. "I feel like I ran into a brick wall."

A minute later, Shannon got up. Coach helped her to the bench, where Shannon stuck an ice pack on her eye. Soon it was halftime, the score 0-0. The Cheetahs had moved the ball across the center stripe only three times. They seemed happy to settle for matching goose eggs. As the Swarm gathered at the bench, Coach Wiffle checked Shannon's eye. "Shan, you've got a nasty shiner coming."

"Shiner?" Shannon repeated.

"Black eye," Coach said. "You're done for the day."

Shannon flung her ice pack into the grass. "No way, Coach. I'm not gonna sit here and watch the Cheetahs play for a tie."

"Shan, Shan, Shan!" the girls chanted.

Coach looked into Shannon's eyes. "You really think you can play?"

"I *know* I can play."

Coach nodded. "Okay, I'll put you back in. But if you look loopy, you're coming out."

Abby raised her hand. "Coach, they have like seven defenders in front of their goal. How do we break through?"

Before Coach could answer, Olga did.

"They've been lucky. Just keep launching balls into the box."

"Olga's right, girls," Coach said. "Sooner or later, the ball will bounce our way."

In the second half the Swarm attacked in waves, but the Cheetahs wouldn't crumble. After their keeper snatched another corner kick, Shannon pulled Abby aside. "Their keeper is a vacuum, we gotta keep the ball away from her. On our next corner, play it ten yards off the far post. "

Three minutes later the Swarm earned a corner kick, and Abby got her chance. Shannon stood near the penalty spot, pinched by two foes. She took four steps toward the near post and then spun toward the back post.

As Shannon measured the arc of Abby's kick, the keeper charged out. Shannon knew it might mean a second black eye, but she jumped and snapped her head into the ball. It flew past the keeper toward the far corner. Shannon felt that first *thump* in her chest, but then a Cheetah dove and headed the ball off the line. Shannon threw her head back. *So close!*

Shannon looked to the sidelines. Her dad held up three fingers. *I gotta do something –*

now. The Cheetah center back blasted the goal kick over the sideline near midfield. As Abby picked up the ball, Shannon knelt. "Rats! Stone in my cleat."

As Shannon untied her left boot and took it off, Abby threw the ball down the line. The two Cheetahs marking Shannon watched Montana chase after it. That's when Shannon made her move. Her boot still off, she sprang out of her crouch and hit top speed in three strides. Glancing back, Shannon saw that she had five yards on her foes.

"Montana, now!" she shouted as she neared the corner of the box. Montana passed into Shannon's path. She ran on and lashed the ball with her right boot, her left boot being thirty yards away. The Cheetah keeper dove. The shot whistled past her hands and poked the net in the far corner.

Shannon ran to Montana and lifted her off the ground. "Great feed, Mon!" she yelled.

"Shan, what you did with your boot, that was wild!" Montana blared.

A minute later, the ref blew her final whistle. Swarm 1, Cheetahs 0. As Shannon reached the bench, Coach wrapped her in a big hug.

"Sensational goal, Shan, but your eye is turning purple."

Coached reached into her cooler and handed Shannon another icepack. "Hold that on your eye, it'll keep the swelling down." As the girls gathered, Coach rested a hand on Shannon's shoulder. "Girls, did you see what Shannon did before she scored?"

"It was crazy," Abby answered. "She unties her boot and takes it off. The two girls marking her look toward the ball. Shannon gets up and bolts off. She left her boot behind – and left those girls in the dust."

"That's right," Coach added, "Shannon untied her boot, and then she untied the game. My word for the day is 'CUNNING.' It means 'skillful in the use of trickery.'"

"Shan, Shan, Shan!" the girls chanted. Shannon grinned under the ice pack. Coach went on. "Girls, we have a big game next Saturday. We play the Monsoon on their field. They lead the league with three wins and no losses. You'll be playing against three of your old teammates – Cat Woods, Tory Smoot, and Chelsea Mills. I'm sure those girls would love to beat us. We gonna let that happen?"

"NO!"

After dinner that night, Shannon took another ice pack to her room. She flopped on her bed and held the pack to her eye for twenty minutes. She got up and looked in the mirror. A purple half-moon sat under her left eye. *Wow, my first black eye, even if it's really purple.*

Shannon opened her computer and checked the league standings.

Team	Wins	Losses	Ties	Points
Monsoon	3	0	0	9
Scorpions	2	0	1	7
Swarm	2	0	1	7
Cheetahs	1	1	1	4
Fury	1	2	0	3
Rampage	1	2	0	3
Galaxy	0	2	1	1
Volcanoes	0	3	0	0

Next, Shannon clicked on the 'Leading Scorers' tab.

Player	Team	Goals	Assists	Points
Swift	Swarm	5	2	12

Bryson	Scorpions	4	3	11
Mills	Monsoon	4	2	10
Smoot	Monsoon	3	3	9

Shannon smiled. *Hope Coach Jack sees this.* She was about to log off when she got a new message. *"Hey loser, who's in first place? Yeah, you lead the league in scoring, but I'll blow past you. Can't wait to play you this Saturday. Swift and the Swarm will eat dirt!"*

Shannon hit reply. *"Hey Chelsea, you know why the Swarm isn't in first place? Some girl missed a penalty kick in our first game!"*

Shannon sent the message. As she expected, she got no reply.

All week, Shannon did her best to avoid Chelsea. Twice she spotted her at a distance in the hall, and both times Shannon ducked into a nearby girls' room. But in geography class on Friday, Mrs. Hooper threw Shannon a curveball. The teacher rose from behind her desk, a ball cap in her hand. "Okay class, time for your first team project," she said. "I've put your names in here.

You'll work in teams of two. I'll pull out two names at a time, and those will be our teams."

Mrs. Hooper went through the first eight pairs without calling Shannon or Chelsea. There were only four names left. Shannon held her breath as the teacher pulled out two more slips. "Shannon and Chelsea," she said, and Shannon felt a shiver dance down her spine.

Mrs. Hooper spent the rest of class going over each assignment with the teams. When she got to Chelsea and Shannon, Chelsea threw up her hands. "Shannon doesn't want to be my partner."

"I never said that!" Shannon shot back.

"Your face says it," Chelsea snapped.

"That's enough, girls," Mrs. Hooper cut in. "Look, you girls love soccer, and flags are important in soccer – the corner flags, the assistant referees' flags. I want you to do a report on the flags of two states. You pick the states. Remember, I want to see you work as a team, and present as a team."

Chelsea opened her phone and did a search. Minutes later, she clicked off and looked at Shannon. "Okay, Swift, I'm doing the flag of Texas. You find some other flag."

"But Chelsea, we're supposed to work together."

"We are," Chelsea retorted. "I do one, and you do one. Together we do two."

"But – "

"Zip it, Swift. Just do your flag, and I'll do mine."

After class ended, Shannon was the last student to leave. A knot in her stomach, she felt trouble lurking. Sure enough, when she reached the hall, Chelsea pounced. "You're goin' down tomorrow, Swift, down hard. You ruined the Swarm, and now I'm gonna ruin you."

Shannon tried to think of a clever response, but came up empty. Chelsea stuck her finger an inch from Shannon's nose. "Scared, huh, Swift? Look, I'm gonna –"

"Back off, girl," Tim broke in as he stepped between the girls. He glared at Chelsea. "You're a bully, Chelsea. Leave Shannon alone."

Chelsea locked eyes with Tim. "Your wimpy sister can't defend herself? Needs her brother to fight her fights?"

"You're just jealous because Shannon owns you at soccer," Tim fired back. He stuck a finger in Chelsea's face, but another hand slapped it away. The hand belonged to Danny Mills, Chelsea's big brother.

"Get outta my sister's face, you punk," Danny ranted. He grabbed Tim by the shirt and pushed him against the lockers. Tim's feet dangled six inches off the ground. Danny growled, "If I see you near my sister again, I'll stuff you in one of these lockers. Got it, boy?"

Tim nodded. Danny dropped him and walked away, Chelsea at his side. Shannon turned to Tim. "Sorry, Tim."

Tim tucked in his shirt. "Wow, I didn't know she had a brother." He frowned. "You gotta fight this battle yourself, Shan. It's the only way you're gonna get through it."

Shannon nodded, her eyes on the floor.

That afternoon, Shannon sprawled on her bed and thought about Tim getting lifted off the floor. *My brother tried to stick up for me, and he got stuck up on the wall.* Her phone rang, Haley. "Hey Shan, I just checked the pumpkins. Their skin is smooth and tough. It's time for us to each pick one and put our names on 'em."

Shannon sprang off her bed. “I’m on my way, Hale.”

Shannon jogged over and met Haley in her backyard. Haley reached in her pocket and held up a long nail. Shannon smiled and followed Haley across the bridge. When they reached the first hill, Shannon’s jaw dropped. “Look how much they’re grown!”

“Okay, Shan, pick one.”

“No way, you get first pick, Hale.”

“There are fifty pumpkins I’d be happy with, Shan. You go first.”

Shannon felt her heart thump as she wandered through the patch. She knelt next to one that was perfectly round, the size of a soccer ball, its skin turning from yellow to light orange. “This is the one, Hale.”

Haley found one like it. Shannon watched as Haley bent down. Holding the nail like a pen, she scratched H-A-L-E. Then she handed the nail to Shannon. “Break the skin, but don’t go too deep,” Haley warned.

Shannon carved S-H-A-N. She noticed some goo oozing out of the letters. “Don’t worry, they always bleed a little,” Haley said. “I’ll come back later and wipe 'em clean. The letters will seal up over night."

"Will our pumpkins get bigger before we take 'em off the vine?" Shannon asked.

"Yep, and as the pumpkins grow, so will our names."

"Cool!"

As the girls walked back toward the house, Haley turned to Shannon. "I am so psyched for tomorrow. The Monsoon are goin' down!"

"Me too," Shannon mumbled. Haley barely heard her. "What's buggin' you, Shan?"

"I think you know, Hale. I mean, what if Chelsea tries to hurt me?"

"Don't think like that, Shan. Remember how you played against her in the tryouts? I mean, you dribbled her cross-eyed."

"Yeah, but that was different. I was worried about making the team."

"Okay, so tomorrow, worry about winning the game. Look, Shan, you gotta get over Chelsea. She's a bully and a brat. We win tomorrow, I bet she never bothers you again."

"You're right, Hale, we're gonna do it."

The girls smacked palms, and Shannon walked home.

Later that night, Shannon tossed in bed. She kept seeing Chelsea's face. She felt the meanness in her eyes, heard the anger in her voice. She got up, walked to the bathroom, and drank a cup of water. Looking in the mirror, Shannon thought about carving her name in the pumpkin. *Today, I put my name in a pumpkin. Tomorrow, I'll put my name in the paper. Right there for Coach Jack to see.*

CHAPTER 9

DIRTY TRICK

AT DAYBREAK SHANNON WOKE TO a noise, but it wasn't her alarm. It was her tummy. She rolled over, but it kept going...a gurgle here, a rumble there. She pulled her blanket tight to her chin. *We have to beat the Monsoon, or Chelsea will hound me forever.*

Hearing the clank of pots and pans, Shannon got up and went down to the kitchen. Her dad was stirring pancake batter. “Dad, I'm a little queasy, not gonna eat now.”

“But you need some fuel for the game.”

“Not hungry, I'll eat later.”

Mr. Swift put a hand on her shoulder. “Don't think about Chelsea, think about your teammates. They need you. You'll play a great game, I know it.”

Shannon sighed. “Hope so, Dad.”

An hour later, Shannon got out of the car at the Monsoon’s field. She looked up at puffy dark clouds inching along. *Those clouds are so low, I feel like I could jump up and touch them.* Trotting toward the field, Shannon watched as a strong gust shook yellow leaves off the trees. As she reached the bench, she told herself not to look over at the Monsoon players, but her eyes didn’t listen. Seeing Chelsea passing with Tory and Cat, Shannon felt another growl in her belly.

A bit later Coach Wiffle called the girls in, but Shannon took off in the other direction. She made the portable bathroom just in time. Even with no breakfast, she got sick. She rinsed her mouth and hustled back to the bench.

“Shan, you okay?” Coach asked.

“Better now, thanks.”

Abby and Montana jogged back from the circle, where they had met the Monsoon captains. “Chelsea and Tory wouldn’t shake our hands,” Abby said. “The ref made ‘em do it.”

Coach clenched her jaw. "Girls, I want this game, you want this game. Let's go get it!"

As Shannon put her hand on the stack of hands, she saw a look in Coach's eyes she'd never seen before. *I've never seen Coach so fired up. We gotta win this game for her.*

The Swarm created the first good chance when Abby cut off a pass and led Montana into the corner. Shannon dashed into the box, her eyes on Montana's cross. As the ball curled in behind her, she knew it was time. *Bicycle kick.* Shannon turned her back toward goal and leaped. But as she swung at the ball, a gust howled. Shannon whiffed, her back thumping on the turf. A defender launched the ball clear, and Chelsea jogged past Shannon. "You and your stupid bicycle kick, hilarious." Shannon opened her mouth, but nothing came out.

In the stands, Mrs. Swift sat on her hands. "Wow, I've never seen her do that."

"It's the wind, Mom, cut her a break," Tim shot back.

Eager to erase her embarrassment, Shannon sprinted back and won a loose ball. She spun away from Tory, but ran smack into Chelsea.

Chelsea made a clean tackle, spilling Shannon into the grass.

"Go, Tor!" Chelsea yelled as she dribbled quickly ahead. When Olga stepped up to challenge, Chelsea and Tory worked a give-and-go around her. Chelsea collected Tory's feed, tapped once, and fired from the edge of the box. Haley dove, but the ball whistled past her and zapped the strings. Monsoon 1, Swarm 0. Chelsea raised her arms and bolted off. She tore up the sideline, nodding at Coach Wiffle as she passed the Swarm bench. Shannon looked at the clouds. *That was my fault, gotta get it back.*

Chelsea and Tory kept Shannon bottled up. She got the ball only a few times, and could do little with it. Neither team could gain an edge, and the half ended with the Monsoon up, 1-0. As Shannon jogged to the sideline, she glanced at her dad. He pumped his fist, and Shannon nodded back. At the bench, chatter grew.

"We're getting beat at midfield," Olga snapped. "Girls, you gotta get back!"

Coach put up her hands. "Relax. Keep the ball on the floor and keep running hard, we'll wear them down."

A minute later, Coach pulled Shannon aside. "You look a little off, wanna take a rest?"

Shannon took that like a slap in the face. "No way, Coach. I'll play better, promise."

When the second half began, Shannon found her stride. Running onto a pass from Abby, she whirled away from Cat and dribbled into space. When Tory challenged, Shannon scissored her legs over the ball. Tory wobbled, and Shannon blew by.

Nearing the corner of the box, Shannon felt Chelsea closing in from the side. Shannon cocked her leg, drawing Chelsea into a slide. But then she cut the ball back along the eighteen, and Chelsea tackled air. Shannon looked up and saw space in the far corner. *Boom*! She laced a knee-high rocket that punched the net inside the far post. Swarm 1, Monsoon 1.

Shannon's teammates swarmed on her, but she was in no mood to celebrate. *Now it's time to win this thing.* For the next ten minutes, Shannon covered the field like the drizzle that had begun to fall. She stole passes, fired potent crosses into the box, and hammered two drives just over the bar.

In the stands, Tim turned to his mom. "I've never seen Shannon so charged up."

Mrs. Swift nodded. "Yeah, she really flipped the switch."

They weren't the only ones to notice. When the ball rolled out of play near midfield, Chelsea called Tory over. "We gotta take out Swift," she said, and Tory nodded.

A bit later, Abby led Shannon into space on the flank. Shannon collected and looked up on Tory and Chelsea, coming at her from different angles. Shannon tried to cut between them, but all three girls merged on the ball. In the tangle of legs, Chelsea jabbed a knee into Shannon's thigh.

"Aargh!" Shannon howled as she dropped to the grass. Tory raced ahead with the ball. Shannon stood, but the knot in her leg pounded. All she could do was limp along and watch. Tory fed wide to wing Layla Tibbs, and Chelsea dashed toward the far post. Layla dribbled to the corner and launched a high cross into the box, and Haley came out and put up her hands.

But Haley didn't jump. Chelsea swooped in, leaped, and stuck her head into the ball before it dropped into Haley's hands. The ball snapped the net under the bar, and Chelsea ran off. This time she skidded on her knees, coming to a stop in front of the Swarm bench. Her teammates piled on.

Coach Wiffle ran out to Shannon. “I’ve got a knot in my thigh,” Shannon said. “Got kneed, can’t walk on it.”

Coach and Abby helped Shannon off the field. Three minutes later, the ref blew the final whistle. Monsoon 2, Swarm 1.

Both teams lined up for handshakes. Shannon stayed on the bench, her hands over her face. Her mom and dad walked over. With one arm around each parent, Shannon hobbled off. A few tears streaked her cheeks. Back in the handshake line, Coach Wiffle came face to face with Chelsea.

“I told ya, Coach,” Chelsea sassed, “you shouldn’t have messed with a good thing.”

Coach Wiffle squeezed hard on Chelsea’s hand. “I saw what you did to Shannon, and I won’t forget it.” Chelsea gave Coach a toothless smile.

By the time Shannon reached the car, her tears had dried.

“How did you get hurt, Shan?” her mom asked.

“Chelsea kneed me, don’t think the ref saw it.”

“That rat is pretty cagey,” Tim snapped. “She knew that three players were coming together on the ball. She figured that was her chance to hurt you and get away with it.”

“How’s your thigh feel now, Shan?” her dad asked.

“It hurts, but the loss hurts more.”

That night, Shannon checked her school notebook. *My geography project is coming up, I gotta choose a flag.* She logged onto her computer and did a search. Shannon glimpsed all fifty flags and read brief descriptions of each one. Finally, she made her decision: South Carolina. She checked a bunch of sites and jotted a rough draft of her presentation. Closing her notebook, she smiled. *Chelsea can have Texas, my flag is much cooler.*

When Shannon woke the next morning, she was afraid to put weight on her leg. When she did, pain stung her thigh. Two hours later at the doctor's office, she learned that she had a deep bruise. No soccer for a week. "Mom, this stinks," Shannon whined as she limped to the car. "I can't play against the Galaxy next Saturday. If we don't win, no way we make it to Washington."

Mrs. Swift shook her head. "Boy, I'd like to go one-on-one with Chelsea Mills."

All week at school, Shannon did her best not to limp. No way was she going to give Chelsea the pleasure. On Friday in geography class, Mrs. Hooper asked each project team to get together. Chelsea didn't move, so Shannon had to walk to the back of the room.

"Your leg doesn't look too bad, Swift," Chelsea cracked. "Bet you'll be able to play next year."

Shannon ignored that. "I'm almost done with my flag report," she said. "What about you?"

"Haven't started it."

"You better get started, we present next week."

"I'll get it done, Swift," Chelsea snapped. "On my schedule, not yours."

The next day, Shannon showed up at the field in jeans and a T-shirt. She felt hollow, sitting inches from the field, knowing that she couldn't help her team. Abby came up to her. "We're gonna win this game for you, Shan."

Shannon smiled. "Thanks, Ab, I know you can do it."

In the first half, Montana set up Abby for three clean strikes inside the box. But each time Abby shot wide or high, and the half ended scoreless. When Abby reached the sideline, Shannon called her over. "You're creating lots of chances, Ab."

"Yeah, but I can't shoot straight," Abby whined.

"No one scores on every shot, Ab. Hey, I noticed something. When you get into shooting range, their keeper cheats way off her line. See if you can chip her."

"Thanks, I'll keep an eye out," Abby said.

For most of the second half, the Swarm pinned the Galaxy in its own end. But with two minutes left, the scoreboard still showed two donuts. Then Abby stole a pass and sped toward the box. Her eyes up, she saw the keeper edging farther off her line. *Here goes.* Abby stubbed her foot under the ball, floating it over the keeper. The keeper backpedaled, leaped, and tipped the ball into the bar. An alert Montana had raced in. She and a defender lunged for the rebound. Montana got her toe to it first, nudging the ball into the net.

Shannon leaped off the bench and punched a fist toward the sky.

The Swarm hung on for a 1-0 victory. They gathered around Coach Wiffle, who rested an arm on Montana's shoulder. "My word for the day is 'OPPORTUNISTIC.' It means, 'taking advantage of opportunities as they arise.' When Abby shot, Montana imagined a rebound. She followed the ball and poked it in. It wasn't pretty, but it was the only way she could beat the defender to it."

"That goal was ugly, Coach," Montana said.

The girls laughed, and Coach held up a hand. "No goal is ugly, girls. Like Coach Jack said, your toes are a weapon. Montana proved it today."

When Shannon got home, she logged on to check the standings. The Monsoon led the league with 13 points. The Swarm and the Scorpions sat tied for second, with 10 points each. *We're still in it.* Shannon checked the schedule. The

Swarm's next game was Saturday against the Volcanoes, the team without a win.

Shannon pressed her knuckles into her thigh. The pain was almost gone. *When we play the Volcanoes, I'll erupt.*

At practice on Tuesday, Shannon ran with no pain. Four days later when the Swarm took the field against the Volcanoes, she was ready. She scored twice and set up another score as the Swarm rolled, 6-1. That night, Shannon logged onto her computer and called up the standings.

Team	w-l-t	Points
Monsoon	4-0-2	14
Scorpions	4-1-1	13
Swarm	4-1-1	13
Fury	3-2-1	10
Cheetahs	2-2-2	6
Rampage	1-3-2	5
Galaxy	1-4-1	4
Volcanoes	0-6-0	0

The Scorpions keep winning. We have to beat them next Saturday, or we won't make the tournament. Next, Shannon hit the 'Leading Scorers' tab.

Player	Team	Goals	Assists	Points
Mills	Monsoon	9	3	21
Swift	Swarm	9	3	21
Bryson	Scorpions	7	3	17
Smoot	Monsoon	7	2	16
Seaver	Fury	5	3	13

Whoa, where did Chelsea come from? An hour later Shannon heard her phone ding, and she opened a new message.

What did I tell you, you little wimp? Monsoon wins the league, I win the scoring title. And then I get to join the Wave. Me, not you! Good luck against the Scorpions next week. I hope you win – so we can crush you in Washington!

Shannon thought about what to write back, but her fingers froze on the keyboard.

CHAPTER 10

SWARM VERSUS SCORPIONS: WHO GETS STUNG?

When Shannon joined Abby and Haley at the lunch table on Monday, she knew something was off. Abby was quiet, her usual smile gone. "Ab, you okay?" Shannon asked.

"The paper mill just shut down," Abby said. "My dad lost his job."

"Oh, Ab, I'm so sorry."

"Yeah, not good," Abby went on. "My mom says we don't have the money for me to go to Washington. If we beat the Scorpions, that is."

Haley put an arm around Abby. "We're gonna beat the Scorpions, Abby. And there's no way we're going to Washington without you."

As the hour ticked by, Abby spoke barely a

word. Shannon had never seen her friend so down.

That night, Shannon trotted next door to try Mr. Punt's newest flavor, Vanilla with Pumpkin Spice. As Mrs. Punt dug out a few scoops, Haley told her about Abby's news. Then Shannon added, "Abby's really sad. I wish we could help her."

Mrs. Punt tapped a finger to her lips. "I have an idea, girls." She held up the ice cream carton and pointed at the smiling pumpkin. "Here's a clue."

Shannon and Haley stared at the pumpkin. Then Haley thumped the table. "We can give our pumpkin money to Abby!"

Shannon broke into a grin. "Great idea, Missus Punt!"

On her way home a bit later, Shannon stepped into a jog. *Abby's not turning into a pumpkin. She's going to Washington!*

When Shannon got home from school on Friday, she spent an hour touching up her flag report. Then she wrote out her plans for the weekend.

Today – pick the two pumpkins with our names, and the pumpkins we'll sell.

Saturday – beat the Scorpions (score at least two goals)

Sunday – sell the pumpkins at Mr. Punt's store, and raise the money for Abby

Shannon read the list. *Wow, this could be the biggest weekend of my life.* Her phone dinged, a text from Haley. *The pumpkins are calling us, let's meet at the shed.* Shannon tapped, *Be over in a flash.* She hustled down to the kitchen, peeled a banana, and tore into it.

Mrs. Swift walked in. "You're inhaling that banana, Shan. Going somewhere?"

"Pumpkin patch," Shannon replied as she headed for the door.

"What about your homework?"

"Almost done."

Shannon bolted out the door and breezed over to Haley's backyard. Haley stepped out of the shed and threw Shannon a pair of gloves. "Okay, Shan, first we'll pick our pumpkins and put 'em aside."

The girls trotted back to the patch and found their pumpkins. Shannon's had grown into a perfect globe. The carved letters were big and bold. “So cool!” Shannon blared. She knelt and turned the pumpkin in her hands. “Will they get more orange, Hale?”

“We’ll put ‘em in the yard, let ‘em cure in the sun,” Haley said. “As they cure, they’ll turn more orange.”

“What do you mean, ‘cure?’” Shannon asked.

“The sun helps ‘em get more ripe.”

“Got it. So how do we get our pumpkins off the vine?”

“Watch this, Shan.” Haley bent over her pumpkin. She eyed the stem, and then she used both hands to snap it off the vine. Haley held the pumpkin up and pointed at the stem, about five inches long. “Try to leave this much stem, Shan. It helps ‘em stay fresh.”

Shannon broke her pumpkin off the vine, and Haley got out her phone. The girls posed, pumpkins in hand, and Haley snapped off a few shots. They carried their pumpkins into the backyard and leaned them against the shed. “Okay, Shan, now we get to gather up the good ones.”

Shannon trailed Haley into the shed. Haley grabbed the wheelbarrow and steered it across the bridge. Each girl chose a hill and began to snap pumpkins free. Soon, the wheelbarrow was full. Haley pushed it up to the deck, where the girls unloaded their haul. In all, they filled the wheelbarrow five times. Daylight had begun to fade when Shannon put the last pumpkin on the deck. Haley counted them up, and pumped her fist.

"Sixty-two pumpkins, best crop ever!" The girls arranged them by size – ten small, thirty-two medium, and twenty large.

Mrs. Punt stepped out with two cups of lemonade. "Nice harvest, girls!" Mrs. Punt handed a cup to each girl. Then she reached into her pocket, pulled out a pencil and pad, and handed them to Haley. "Do the math, Haley."

Haley scribbled some numbers. *Ten times three. Thirty-two times five. Twenty times seven.* Haley faced Shannon. "If we sell 'em all, that's three hundred and thirty dollars."

"That's more than Abby needs!" Shannon blurted.

The girls finished their lemonades, and then Shannon left. She broke into a jog, and didn't stop until she found her mom at the kitchen table.

“How many pumpkins you pick?” Mrs. Swift asked.

“Sixty-two, and if we sell ‘em, we can pay Abby’s way to Washington.”

“If you go to Washington,” Mrs. Swift said. “You ready to sting the Scorpions tomorrow?”

“I better be, biggest game of my life.”

“You’re tied with Chelsea, nine goals each,” her mom followed. “You score a few tomorrow, you could win the scoring title. Coach Jack would notice that.”

“I know, Mom. Hope I can fill the net.”

Shannon went upstairs. She thought about her pumpkin, sitting in the grass in Haley’s backyard. *Today, I picked the best pumpkin in the patch. Tomorrow, I’ll be the best player on the pitch.*

In the pre-game huddle at Freedom Park the next day, Coach Wiffle shared some big news. “The Monsoon rallied to beat the Fury this morning, two to one. And guess what? Chelsea Mills scored two goals in the last two minutes. So the Monsoon has earned one spot in Washington. We’re tied for second with the

Scorpions. That means we must win today to earn the other spot." Coach paused and ran her eyes across each girl. "Do we want another shot at the Monsoon?"

"YES!"

Coach stuck out a hand and the girls piled theirs on top. "Swarm, Swarm, Swarm!" As Shannon jogged onto the field, she felt distracted. Chelsea wasn't there, but she was in her head. Shannon knew she was two goals behind in the scoring race. *I can't let that girl beat me.*

Four minutes in, Shannon flagged a loose ball thirty yards from goal. Abby ran free to her left, but Shannon was set on the net. She tried to slither between two foes, but the ball got tackled away.

Abby jogged over. "I was open, Shan." Shannon nodded, but said nothing. A few minutes later, Shannon latched onto a loose ball just outside the Scorpions' box. Montana cut into space and called for the ball, but Shannon dribbled once and fired over the bar.

Montana ran over. "Shan, you had me."

"I had a good look," Shannon shot back.

In the stands, Tim tapped his feet on the

cement. "Shannon's trying to be the hero. She's gotta pass the ball!"

"She's gonna score, I can feel it," Mrs. Swift said.

"She doesn't have to score, Mom. Her *team* has to score."

Later, Shannon ran down a stray pass in the circle. She spun, but right into a cluster of three Scorpions. Olga called for a back pass, but Shannon bulled ahead. She eluded the first two opponents, but the third stripped the ball clean. This time, Shannon's selfish play would cost the Swarm.

The Scorpion passed wide to her left wing. The wing tried to cross, but she mis-hit the ball. It was a lucky flub. The ball sailed over Haley, hit the back post, and caromed into the net. As Shannon jogged back to her spot, she could feel Olga's eyes burning through her. *Okay, I screwed up, but I'll make up for it.* The half ended with the Scorpions ahead, 1-0.

As Shannon reached the sideline, Coach Wiffle pulled her aside. "You're trying to do it all yourself," Coach said. "Your teammates are running into space. You've got to reward them with the ball." Shannon nodded, her eyes on the turf. *I don't need to win the scoring title. We need to win this game.*

Early in the second half, a Scorpion went down with an injury. With play halted, Coach called in Shannon and Abby. "The back post is open on our corner kicks. On our next one, Shannon will fake near post and circle to the back."

"Good idea," Abby said. "It's a narrow field, so I can reach the far post."

A bit later, the Swarm earned a corner kick. Shannon ran toward the near post but then swung around toward the back. She turned to see Abby's kick coming right at her. As the keeper neared, Shannon jumped. She snapped her forehead into the ball, just before the keeper got her mitts on it. The ball flew clean into the net, tying the game, 1-1. Shannon sprinted back to her position, her mind already on the next goal.

As the clock ticked down, neither team could scare the frame. When the Swarm got a throw-in near the center stripe, Shannon picked up the ball and looked at her dad. He held up two fingers. *I gotta do something, now. We don't want to go to penalty kicks.*

Montana bolted down the flank, and Shannon threw ahead of her. As Montana collected Shannon ran into space, and Montana played the ball into her path. She gathered at full speed, blew past a defender, and neared the corner of the box. Glancing up, Shannon saw a gap at the near post, Abby running free toward the far post.

Shannon was torn. *Should I shoot, or try to set up Abby?* She chipped the ball into Abby's path. It sailed over the keeper and drifted down a few yards off the far post. Abby ran on and dove, her body parallel to the ground and three feet above it. Sailing like a dart, Abby met the ball with her forehead.

The ball flew into the net – and so did Abby. Shannon was the third player into the pile, and soon the entire team had buried Abby. The Swarm held off the Scorpions to earn a 2-1 win – and a trip to Washington.

Coach called the girls in. She was about to speak when Shannon and Abby snuck up behind her and dumped a bucket of ice cubes on her head. "Aaah!" Coach yelped. She shook her sweatshirt, a few cubes spilling out. "Girls, my word for today is, 'WASHINGTON.'" The girls howled, and Coach went on. "There are four teams in our bracket. If we win our first two games, we make the championship game."

Shannon's mind was already on Chelsea. "When do we play the Monsoon?" she asked.

"They're in the other bracket," Coach said. "If we play them, it would be in the final."

"Bring on the Monsoon!" Abby yelled. Coach put up a hand. "One more thing, girls. My friend's cousin works at the White House. He's going to arrange a private tour for us."

"Too cool!" Haley yelled.

As the girls started to walk off, Shannon and Haley nodded at each other. They hustled to catch up with Abby. "You scored a great goal, Ab," Haley said.

"Thanks, Hale," Abby replied. "I won't be going to Washington, but at least you guys will."

Shannon wrapped an arm around Abby. "Promise us one thing, Ab. Don't make any plans for next weekend, okay?"

Abby squinted. "What do you mean?"

"You'll see," Haley said.

In the parking lot, Shannon dished out three high-fives. "Your pass to Abby was a gem," Mr.

Swift said. Shannon smiled. “I was about to shoot, but I figured Abby had a better chance.”

“You made the right call,” Tim commented. “Good thing, too, because you hogged the ball the whole first half.”

“You’re right Tim, I was obsessed with the scoring title. At half time, Coach woke me up.”

“You earned your first trip to Washington, Shan,” Mrs. Swift said.

“Yeah, and tomorrow Haley and I gotta make sure Abby is going with us.”

Riding home, Shannon thought about Coach’s message at halftime. *I learned a lesson today. I can never put myself ahead of my team.*

CHAPTER 11

MRS. HOOPER MAKES A GREAT SAVE

LATER THAT AFTERNOON, SHANNON WAS napping on the couch when the doorbell stirred her. Seeing Haley on the porch, Shannon sprang up and opened the door. Haley held a folder in one hand, a brown bag in the other. She handed the folder to Shannon. "These are for you, my dad printed them at his store."

Shannon pulled out two color photos made from the selfies Haley took in the pumpkin patch. Looking at one, she said, "It's funny, Hale, our pumpkins could be twins."

"Not quite, I measured. Yours is a half-inch taller. But we're even, because my stem is a half-inch longer."

Haley held out the brown bag. "My mom

bought those to give out at Halloween, but I don't want them in the house."

Shannon peeked in at a pile of Butterfinger bars. "I love Butterfingers, but you should keep 'em."

Haley waved a finger. "Think about it, Shan. Butterfingers in a goalkeeper's house?"

Shannon snickered at that. Haley took a sheet of paper from her pocket. "Okay, time to get serious. Here's our plan for tomorrow." Haley read: "Load the pumpkins in the car at two o'clock. Go to the store and set up. Sell sixty-two pumpkins – and get Abby to Washington!! Come home and celebrate -- with two kinds of ice cream."

Shannon pumped a fist. "Can't wait, Hale." As Haley headed for home, Shannon watched her stroll across the yard. *I get a real kick out of Haley Punt. Hey, that was a good one!*

That night, Shannon checked her email before going to bed. She opened the only message. *So the wimp is going to Washington, huh? Too bad your trip will be ruined by a Monsoon!*

Shannon hit 'delete.' *Chelsea Mills, I can't get away from that brat. In two days, we present on flags in geography class. And then we might play each other in Washington.*

The next day, Haley and Shannon loaded the pumpkins into the Punts' van. As Mrs. Punt drove the girls to the store, Shannon nibbled her lip. "Hope we sell 'em all, for Abby."

"Don't worry, my dad's been telling all his customers."

Mrs. Punt pulled into the lot and found a space near the store. She and the girls lugged up the nine baskets of pumpkins and set them on a huge table under the storefront awning. Haley taped a sign to the window: JUST-PICKED PUMPKINS – $3, $5, $7.

Mrs. Punt got out her purse. "Okay, let's get this party started. I'll take one pumpkin from each basket." She plunked down fifteen dollars.

"You're awesome, Missus Punt!" Shannon blared. But then she had a thought. "Missus Punt, these pumpkins are from your patch. You don't need to buy them."

"Ah, but Haley and you raised them, Shannon," Mrs. Punt said.

Over the next few hours, customers beat a

steady path to the table. Haley counted. The girls had sold forty-two pumpkins. But just like that, their luck changed. A long rumble of thunder rang out. Dark clouds swept in, and the first few drops splattered the pavement. The clouds sat parked, and the drops came bigger and faster. “It’s raining marbles,” Haley whined. Shannon nodded. “Yeah, never seen it come down so hard.”

Customers leaving the store had no time for pumpkins; they scurried straight for their cars. Soon it was nearly six o’clock, closing time. Haley looked at Shannon. “I can’t believe this, it’s never happened before.”

Shannon counted up the unsold pumpkins – twenty. “Sorry, Hale. I must be bad luck.”

“This isn’t on you, Shan. Blame Mother Nature.”

Haley called her mom to arrange a ride home. A bit later a car pulled in, but it wasn’t Mrs. Punt’s. The girls saw a woman get out, an umbrella hiding her head. As the woman trotted closer, Shannon felt her heart race. *I think I know her.*

The woman hustled under the awning and

lowered her umbrella. Shannon's jaw fell open. "Missus Hooper!" she blared.

"I'm so glad you're still here, girls," Mrs. Hooper said. "I need pumpkins for a class project next week. How many do you have left?"

"Twenty," Haley said.

"Perfect, I'll take 'em all."

Shannon's jaw dropped. "Missus Hooper, you're the greatest!"

The girls helped load the pumpkins into the back of Mrs. Hooper's car. They were pelted by drops the size of nickels, but they didn't feel a thing. Once the last basket was loaded, they scrambled back under the awning. Haley counted the money. "Three hundred and thirty dollars, that's the most ever! Abby is going to Washington!" The girls agreed that they would tell Abby after practice the next day, so all their teammates could celebrate together.

Before practice on Monday, Haley and Shannon shared their news with Coach Wiffle. Two hours later, Coach ended the scrimmage and called the team in. "Girls, Haley and Shannon have some news to share."

Coach nodded at Haley, and she spoke. “Shannon and I sold sixty-two pumpkins yesterday and raised over three hundred dollars.” She looked at Abby. “Ab, that means you’re going to Washington.”

As the girls cheered, tears sprang to Abby’s eyes. She hugged Haley and then Shannon, and Shannon felt a tear dribble out.

Tuesday, flag day for Shannon. As she settled into her seat in geography class that afternoon, she could feel her heart hammer. Half way through class, Mrs. Hooper called Shannon and Chelsea to the front. The girls walked up and stood side by side, neither looking at the other. Chelsea went first. “I chose the state flag of Texas,” she began. “Texas is known as the Lone Star state. Its flag has only one star, and that star stands for Texas. The colors are red, white and blue, the same as our country’s flag. The white stands for purity, the blue is for loyalty, and the red is for bravery.”

After Chelsea finished, Mrs. Hooper asked her why she chose the Texas flag over all the others.

“Easy, Missus Hooper. The flag is like me. There’s one star on it. When I play soccer, there's only one star on the field." Groans filled the room.

Shannon was next. "I chose the flag of South Carolina. It has two images – a crescent and a palmetto tree. Each image tells something about the state's history. The crescent looks like a moon, but it really represents a silver emblem that was placed on the caps of soldiers who fought against the British in the Revolutionary War."

Shannon paused for a peek at her notes. "The palmetto tree was like a secret weapon in that war. The British Navy tried to attack the city of Charleston. The American soldiers built a fort. But the fort's walls were not made of stone, they were made of palmetto trees. When the British fired cannonballs at the fort, they just bounced off the trees. The fort survived."

After Shannon finished, Mrs. Hooper asked her why she chose the South Carolina flag. "It's such a simple image, you could draw it from your memory," Shannon said. "Lots of state flags have so many words and images that you can't really focus on anything."

Mrs. Hooper turned to the class. "Any comments on these flags?"

Abby raised her hand. “I like the single star on the Texas flag,” she said. “But when I think of that star, I think of Shannon, not Chelsea.”

Chatter ran through the room. Chelsea glared at Abby. “You little punk,” Chelsea snorted. “I’m gonna –”

“That’s enough!” Mrs. Hooper bellowed, her voice raised for the first time that Shannon could remember. After class ended, Shannon caught up to Abby in the hall. “Ab, what you said about the star, that was wild.”

“Yeah, pretty funny. You see Missus Hooper? She was trying to cover her smile.”

“But the best part was Chelsea’s reaction,” Shannon said. “That’s the first time I’ve seen her face match the color of her hair.”

On Friday morning, Shannon, her teammates, and several family members gathered at Freedom Park. In all, there were eight cars in the caravan heading to Washington D.C. They rode through Delaware and Maryland, and three hours later they reached the garage of their hotel. After they checked in, Coach Wiffle led the girls and their family members on the short walk to the White House. As they neared the front gate, a tall young man with short blond hair met them with a smile. Coach Wiffle greeted the man. He introduced himself as Jeff, and then each girl introduced herself by name.

"I'm excited to show you the White House," Jeff began. "But before we go in, let's start with a question right here. Who can name the tallest structure in Washington?"

No one answered. "I'll give you a clue," Jeff said. "You can see it."

Abby followed Jeff's gaze to a thin brick building jutting high into the sky. She put up a hand. "The Washington Monument?" she guessed.

"One point for Abby," Jeff said. He pointed to the monument. "That rises five hundred and sixty feet. That's about two soccer fields stacked on top of one another."

Jeff led the groups toward the White House. Inside, they cleared a security station, and then Jeff led them to a portrait of Abraham Lincoln. "President Lincoln would sometimes go to meetings without a briefcase," he said. "Any idea where he kept his papers?"

"In his pocket?" Shannon guessed.

"Good try. Lincoln wore what was called a stovepipe hat. It was tall and thin, and his papers fit in it. Lincoln himself was tall, six feet, four inches. His hat made him look more than seven feet tall. That's almost as high as a soccer crossbar."

Haley put up a hand. "Do you think I could wear a stovepipe hat in goal?"

Jeff smiled at that one. He led the girls down the hall to another portrait. "William Harrison served as president for only thirty-two days," Jeff said. "He died from pneumonia he caught while standing in the cold when he was sworn into office."

Jeff turned the corner and came to another portrait. "Andrew Jackson didn't learn to read until he was seventeen years old. His parents couldn't afford to send him to school."

Shannon shook her head. *And then he went on to become president, that's unreal.*

Next, the girls followed Jeff into a huge room. "This is the East Room," he said. "President Roosevelt let his kids roller skate in here."

Abby raised a hand. "How many rooms are in this place?"

"The White House has a hundred and thirty-two rooms," Jeff answered.

"Wow," Abby said, "you could have a wild game of hide-and-seek."

Jeff led the group into the backyard, where he pointed at an old tree house built into a large oak. "President Jimmy Carter made that tree house for his daughter, Amy. She used to watch special ceremonies from there. No one even knew she was there."

Suddenly two dogs ran into the yard, pawing playfully at each other. Jeff pointed at them. "Over the years, the White House has doubled as a zoo," he said. "All but two presidents keep pets here."

"What kind of pets?" Shannon asked.

"Lyndon Johnson had two beagles," Jeff said. "They were named, 'Him' and 'Her.' President Coolidge had two lion cubs, a donkey, a wallaby, and a pygmy hippo."

"A pygmy hippo?" Abby repeated.

"It's a small hippopotamus, but shaped more like a pig," Jeff explained.

"I read about that pygmy hippo," Abby said. "Its name was, 'Chelsea.'"

The girls hooted, and Jeff went on. "John

Quincy Adams kept an alligator in the White House. Benjamin Harrison had a goat named, 'Old Whiskers.' William Taft had a cow named, 'Pauline.' He drank milk from Pauline. And Zachary Taylor brought his horse to the White House. It would eat the grass on the front lawn, drove the yard crew crazy."

"That's funny," Abby cracked, "because this weekend, Chelsea's gonna be eating grass." The girls whooped again.

Over dinner in the hotel's restaurant that night, Coach asked each girl to name her favorite part of the White House. After the girls had finished, Shannon raised a hand. "There was one thing about the White House that bugged me," she said.

"What was that?" Coach asked.

"It was a message on a plaque. It was written by John Quincy Adams, the second president. I wrote it in my phone notes."

"Why don't you read it?" Coach said.

Shannon stood, her phone in hand. "It said, '*May none but honest and wise men rule this roof.*'"

"What don't you like about that, Shan?" Coach asked.

"Come on, Coach. Wise men? What about wise women?"

The chant began to grow. "Shan, Shan, Shan!"

Coach put up her hand. "Shannon, you make a good point. But back then, women didn't hold positions of power. They weren't even able to vote."

"Yeah, well, look at us now," Haley snapped. "We can't be stopped."

"Swarm, Swarm, Swarm!" cheered the girls.

On Saturday, the Swarm won both their games. Shannon scored the winning goal in each match. The Monsoon won both their matches, too. The stage was set for a showdown on Sunday: Swarm versus Monsoon. Shannon versus Chelsea.

After dinner that night, Coach Wiffle pulled Shannon aside. "I'm making you captain tomorrow."

Shannon crinkled her nose. "But it's not my turn."

“You’ve earned it, Shan. I know you’re gonna play the game of your life.”

When Shannon got to her room, she heard her phone beep. She found an email from Chelsea. She hit “delete” without reading it, and crawled into bed. *I’ll answer that message on the field tomorrow.*

CHAPTER 12

REMATCH: SWARM VERSUS MONSOON

UNDER A BRIGHT SUN AT noon the next day, the referee blew his whistle and called for captains. As Shannon trotted toward the circle, she looked at the Monsoon huddle. Out of it jogged Chelsea. In the circle, the girls came face to face.

"You look like sisters," the ref said.

"Hah!" Chelsea snapped. "Don't insult me."

"That was no insult," the ref fired back. "Now shake hands."

Shannon put out her hand and Chelsea shook it hard, her mean eyes boring in. Shannon stared back, not one blink. She won the coin toss and jogged back to the huddle. Coach Wiffle put out her hand and the girls stacked theirs on top. Coach clenched her teeth. "Girls, this team cheated us once. Now it's payback time. One, two, three...Swarm, Swarm, Swarm!"

Shannon took the field, her pulse hammering. But this time it hammered out of passion, not fear. A passion to win, a passion to silence Chelsea Mills. Soon after the opening whistle, the Monsoon won a throw-in. As Cat threw down the line to Tory, Chelsea and Shannon jogged side by side. Chelsea saw the ref follow the ball, and then she stepped on Shannon's toes and took off. Shannon ran after Chelsea, but a bolt of pain shot through her foot.

"Now!" Chelsea yelled as she neared the box.

Tory pushed the ball into Chelsea's path. She gathered in the arc, Shannon bearing down from behind. Chelsea tapped once and swung her boot into the ball. Shannon slid, but she was a split second late. The Swarm was about to get hit with a double-whammy. First, as Chelsea tumbled over Shannon, her shot sizzled past Haley and curled into the corner. Second, while Chelsea got mobbed by her teammates, the ref called Shannon over. "That's was a reckless slide, eleven." He pulled out a yellow card and held it over Shannon.

"But ref, she stepped on my foot."

The ref ran off. Shannon bit her lip. *Great, the game is barely five minutes old. We're behind, and I have a card.*

"Let's get it back, Swarm!" yelled Coach Wiffle.

A minute later, Chelsea made trouble again. She stole a pass intended for Shannon and charged ahead. When Abby stepped up, Chelsea poked the ball between her legs. "Get on her, Abby!" Coach screamed.

But Abby was no match for Chelsea's long legs. For every two strides Chelsea took, Abby needed three. As Chelsea neared the box, Olga challenged. Chelsea dipped her shoulder left and nudged the ball to the right. Olga was caught leaning the wrong way, giving Chelsea a clear shot at net. Chelsea cracked a low drive. Haley dove and tipped the ball just wide. Shannon saw Chelsea's entire run – she was seven yards behind her the whole way. *Wow, Chelsea is even faster than I remember.*

"Shannon, get over here!" Coach Wiffle hollered. Shannon sprinted to the bench. "You need to smother Chelsea. Don't let her touch the ball."

Shannon ran back and headed the corner

kick out of the box. Montana controlled and dribbled ahead. She looked for Shannon, but Chelsea was on her like a second shirt. Montana tried to beat Tory, but Tory tackled the ball away. "Tory, now!" Chelsea yelled as she darted away from Shannon.

Tory led Chelsea up the middle. Chelsea collected and built speed toward the box, with Shannon, Olga, and Montana giving chase. Out of the corner of her eye, Chelsea saw Cat run free on her right. Without looking, Chelsea fed Cat at the corner of the box. As Cat broke in alone, Haley charged off her line. Cat cocked her leg, dropping Haley to her knees. Cat cut around her and pushed the ball toward the goal. Olga slid, but she was too late. Monsoon 2, Swarm 0.

Chelsea ran over and lifted Cat in the air. Shannon turned her back on the celebration. *I gotta wake up, now.* In the stands, Mrs. Swift hung her head. "This is hard to watch, Tim. They come this far, and they play this bad."

"Stop whining, Mom," Tim retorted. "They have time to come back."

When the whistle sounded for halftime, the Swarm jogged off in a two-goal hole. "Girls, we're just watching!" Coach Wiffle railed. "Assert yourselves! Come on, one goal and we're back in it."

A bit later Shannon took the field with a new plan. *My teammates can't find me, so I have to find the ball.* In the third minute, Tory gathered a loose ball in the circle. Shannon saw Chelsea twenty yards behind Tory. *Now's my chance.* Shannon raced after Tory, swooped in from behind, and swept the ball off her boot.

Feeling Chelsea on her heels, Shannon flicked to Abby, who swung the ball ahead of Montana toward the far corner. Montana ran on and sent a long ball toward the back post. Shannon beat Chelsea to the cross and cushioned it on her chest fifteen yards from goal. Chelsea caught up and faced Shannon. "Come on, girl, try me," Chelsea sassed.

Shannon spied Olga running free toward the arc. She rolled a soft pass into Olga's path, and Olga thumped her right instep into it. The keeper could only watch as the shot skittered into the far corner. Monsoon 2, Swarm 1. "That's one!" Olga screamed as she raced over and leaped into Shannon's arms.

Just like that, the momentum swung. The

Swarm won loose balls and strung passes together. But the Monsoon moved a midfielder to the back line. They played to protect the lead, lumping out one aimless ball after another. After Abby fired over the bar from twenty-five yards, Shannon looked to the sidelines. Mr. Swift held up seven fingers. *Seven minutes left, it's time to make something happen.*

Chelsea controlled the goal kick. She tapped to Tory and bolted up the flank, Shannon close behind. Tory tried to pass back to Chelsea, but Shannon slid in and knocked the ball out of play. Chelsea glared at Shannon. "You're goin' down, Swift."

Shannon glared back, but fought off the urge to respond. Tory threw toward Chelsea, but Shannon stepped in and smashed the ball high into the Monsoon half. As Abby chased it down, Shannon hit top speed across the stripe. Chelsea was bent over and out of breath. "Get Swift!" she yelled. Abby pushed the ball ahead of Shannon, thirty yards from goal. When a defender neared, Shannon dazed her with a few scissors moves and broke free near the corner of the box.

As Cat neared, Shannon unleashed. It was

a blistering drive, the ball rising six feet before leveling off. Shannon watched the keeper take one step and dive. The ball sailed over her hands and popped the strings in the far corner. Swarm 2, Monsoon 2. Shannon tried to run but Abby tackled her and Montana jumped into the pile. As the Swarm huddled around their star, Shannon spoke. “Girls, they’re tired, we can outrun them.”

But Chelsea had found her second wind. She took the kick-off, tapped the ball between Shannon’s boots, and gathered speed. When Olga stepped up to challenge, Chelsea leaned right but cut left. Olga wobbled, and Chelsea broke free near the eighteen. Haley rushed out to shrink Chelsea’s shooting angles, but Chelsea weaved around her and took aim at the open goal. Shannon was hustling back. As Chelsea swung into the ball, Shannon slid. She deflected the shot, sending it inches outside the near post. Chelsea fell hard.

“Where’s the foul?” Chelsea cried from her knees. “That should be her second card!”

“She got the ball first!” yelled the ref.

Shannon headed the corner kick out to Montana on the flank. When Montana bolted past Cat, Shannon accelerated. Chelsea was out of gas. She looked at the ref, his eyes on the ball. As Shannon ran past, Chelsea jabbed an elbow into her stomach. "Aaahh!" Shannon shrieked as she crumpled to the grass.

The ref blew his whistle. He jogged over and huddled with his assistant. The ref turned and pointed at Chelsea. "You, get over here."

"But she tripped!" Chelsea hollered as she walked toward the ref. He reached into his book and pulled out a card. A red card.

"But I didn't do anything!" Chelsea wailed.

"My assistant saw it all," the ref shot back. "Get off the field, now."

Her head down, Chelsea dragged her feet toward the sideline. Shannon got up and looked at her dad, who held up one finger. *Gotta do it now.*

Abby ran over. "You okay, Shan?"

"Just get me the ball."

Olga played the free kick to Montana, who blazed down the flank. On the other side, Shannon was finally free of Chelsea. She sprinted toward the goal, reaching the box just as Montana floated a cross toward the far post. Shannon slowed, the ball curling in behind her.

She knew this was her chance. *Time to get in gear.* She slowed, turned her back to the goal and leaped. Leaning back in midair, Shannon swung her left leg up and then swept her right boot at the ball. *Thump*! The strike was pure.

Shannon crashed to the turf, her eyes looking away from the goal. The keeper never moved. For a second, a stunned silence hung over the field. Shannon didn't see it, but her bicycle kick had arched over the keeper and dipped under the bar. Shannon rolled over and saw the ball in the net. She sprang up and ran past the Monsoon bench, waving her arms. When she reached her half, Haley tackled her and her teammates piled on.

The girls kept celebrating, until the ref looked at his watch. "Let's get on with it!" he yelled.

The Swarm players started walking slowly onto the field. Finally, the ref's patience expired. He put the ball down and backed out of the circle. "Get back in position!" Coach Wiffle yelled.

As Shannon and her teammates ran across the field, the ref blew his whistle. Cat tapped to Tory, who took off toward the unguarded net.

Haley led her teammates in frantic pursuit. As Haley closed in, Tory let fly from thirty yards. The ball bounced once, struck the post, and kicked back into the goalmouth. Tory and Haley raced, neck and neck. Tory lunged at the ball, but Haley dove and punched it away. The final whistle sounded. Swarm 3, Monsoon 2.

Shannon dropped to her back and stared at the sky. Montana and Abby dove on her. Before long, the whole team had swarmed into a heap. "Shan, that was the greatest goal I've ever seen!" Abby shouted. "Even better than the one you scored at your tryout."

"I wish I'd seen it," Shannon cracked.

"Hey," Montana whispered, "check out the Monsoon bench." Shannon looked over. Chelsea was crying into a towel. Tory had buried her face inside her shirt. Cat was nowhere to be seen. Shannon got back on her feet, and she and Haley hugged.

"Shan, we did it."

"Thanks for everything, Hale," Shannon said, a tear in her eye.

"What did I do, Shan?"

"You've been my friend, from the day I moved here."

Haley smiled. "Shan, being your friend is the easiest thing I've ever done."

Coach Wiffle called the girls over. "Girls, my word for the day is 'CHAMPIONS,'" she said, her voice hoarse. "You came from two goals down. You believed in yourselves. You earned this title."

"Coach, why did the ref put the ball in play before we were ready?" Abby asked.

"Because you were celebrating in your own half," Coach said. "The ref had every right to do that. We almost blew it, but I've never seen Haley run that fast."

Haley smiled. "No way was I gonna let Tory beat me to that ball."

The girls posed for pictures at midfield. As Shannon walked back toward the bench, she saw Chelsea walking toward her. "I'll be back, Swift," Chelsea vowed. "And I'll prove that I'm the best player in Manchester. Me, not you."

Shannon stared into Chelsea's eyes. "Chelsea, I don't care about being the best player. I just want to play for the best team."

Shannon waited for a response. For once, Chelsea had nothing to say. She even gave Shannon a slight nod. Then she turned and walked off. Shannon met her family behind the bench, and her dad lifted her off the ground. “I’m so proud of you, Shan,” he raved. “When the team needed you, you came through.”

“Thanks, Dad.”

Mrs. Swift hugged Shannon next. “Shan, you stood up to Chelsea Mills.”

“You did it when you were my age, Mom. Today, it was my turn.”

Tim put out his fist, and Shannon tapped it. “Shan, that last goal was crazy. Forget about the thirty bucks you owe me. Just teach me that bicycle kick.”

Shannon laughed. As she picked up her bag, she noticed a man walking toward her. He wore a black track suit over black sneakers. Jack Dash, the man in black, the coach of the Wave. “Shannon, could I speak with you for second?” he asked.

Shannon looked at her dad, and he nodded. Her heart beating fast, Shannon followed Coach Dash toward the circle. They stood, eye to eye. “I just realized that I’ve been scouting the wrong player,” Coach Dash said. “I want you to join my team.”

Shannon's jaw fell open. "Uh, thanks, but I like my team."

"I'm sure you do," Coach Dash said. "But my team plays all over the world. This spring, we're going to Italy and England for tournaments."

"Wow, that sounds cool."

Coach Dash gave Shannon a card with his number on it. "I don't need an answer now. Just promise me you'll think about it, okay?"

"Okay," Shannon said.

Coach Dash smiled and walked off. Shannon jogged toward her family. She knew she had a big decision to make, but it didn't matter. *This is the best day of my life.*

ACKNOWLEDGEMENTS

My parents, Bob and Dorothy Summers, took me to England at age six and introduced me to the greatest game on earth. Laurie Summers, my dear spouse, reviewed several drafts and made each one better. My children, Kate, John, and Caroline, provided helpful insights. My sisters-in-law, Anne Hayden and Dee Mitchell, gave me constructive observations. My brother, Rob, his spouse, Corie, and their two older daughters, Kaia Summers and Ruby Summers, were a steady source of inspiration. Kaia and Ruby read the manuscript, asked lots of thoughtful questions, and even straightened me out a few times. Those conversations alone made writing the book worthwhile.

ABOUT THE AUTHOR

Bill Summers is a soccer author, journalist, player, and coach. He is the author of the Shannon Swift Soccer Series for girls, featuring *Magic Boots*, *Scuffed Boots* (coming soon), and *Buffed Boots* (coming soon). Summers has also written the Max Miles Soccer Series for boys, made up of *Clash of Cleats*, *Cracked Cleats* (coming soon), and *Comeback Cleats* (coming soon). Summers is the author of the young-adult novel, *Red Card*. His book on coaching, *The Soccer Starter*, was published by McFarland & Company. As a parent, Summers coached boys' and girls' youth teams for over a decade. He was captain of the men's soccer team at Cornell University, where he earned his degree in Communication Arts. To learn more, visit:

www.billsummersbooks.com.

Coming this fall...

SCUFFED BOOTS

HERE'S A SNEAK PREVIEW:

SHANNON SWIFT KNEW THE CLOCK was running out.

Her head on her pillow, Shannon ran her eyes over the long crack on her ceiling. *I'm like my ceiling – cracking apart. How can something I love so much make me stress out so bad?*

Two soccer teams wanted Shannon. She could choose only one. She loved playing for the Swarm, her town travel team. But now Shannon had an offer to join the Wave, the best under-thirteen academy team in New Jersey. She checked her watch: 3:17. She had less than two hours to decide.

Shannon closed her eyes and drifted off, but her phone rattled her. A text from Haley

Punt, her best friend, next-door-neighbor, and Swarm teammate. *Wanna fire some shots at me?* Shannon tapped, *Meet ya out back in five.* She bundled her long red hair in a ponytail and changed into her soccer gear. Hopping down the stairs two at a time, she stepped onto the deck and grabbed a ball from the bin. A light mist dotted Shannon's face as she trotted onto the Square, the mini soccer field in her backyard. She was eleven touches into a juggle when she heard the gate jiggle.

Haley walked in, but she wasn't alone. Behind her marched in every one of Shannon's teammates. At the back, Abby Rains and Montana West held a banner that read, *Swift and the Swarm – a Perfect Match.* Under the words, Abby had drawn a picture of Shannon in mid-air whacking her favorite shot – a bicycle kick. The girls began to chant. "Shannon... *Swarm!* Shannon... *Swarm!*"

Made in the USA
Las Vegas, NV
16 October 2021

32483145R00099